**TEACHER'S PET PUBLICATIONS**

LITPLAN TEACHER PACK
for
White Fang
based on the book by
Jack London

Written by
Mary B. Collins

© 1996 Teacher's Pet Publications
All Rights Reserved

This **LitPlan** for Jack London's
White Fang
has been brought to you by Teacher's Pet Publications, Inc.

Copyright Teacher's Pet Publications 1996
11504 Hammock Point
Berlin MD 21811

Only the student materials in this unit plan (such as worksheets,
study questions, and tests) may be reproduced multiple times
for use in the purchaser's classroom.

For any additional copyright questions,
contact Teacher's Pet Publications.

www.tpet.com

TABLE OF CONTENTS - *White Fang*

Introduction	5
Unit Objectives	8
Reading Assignment Sheet	9
Unit Outline	10
Study Questions (Short Answer)	13
Quiz/Study Questions (Multiple Choice)	24
Pre-reading Vocabulary Worksheets	43
Lesson One (Introductory Lesson)	61
Nonfiction Assignment Sheet	63
Oral Reading Evaluation Form	65
Writing Assignment 1	68
Writing Assignment 2	75
Writing Assignment 3	77
Writing Evaluation Form	79
Vocabulary Review Activities	73
Extra Writing Assignments/Discussion ?s	71
Unit Review Activities	81
Unit Tests	85
Unit Resource Materials	117
Vocabulary Resource Materials	133

A FEW NOTES ABOUT THE AUTHOR
JACK LONDON

LONDON, Jack (1876-1916). The novelist and short-story writer Jack London was, in his lifetime, one of the most popular authors in the world. After World War I his fame was eclipsed in the United States by a new generation of writers, but he remained popular in many other countries, especially in the Soviet Union, for his romantic tales of adventure and survival.

John Griffith London was born in San Francisco on Jan. 12, 1876. His family was poor, and he was forced to go to work early in life to support himself. At 17 he sailed to Japan and Siberia on a seal-hunting voyage. He was largely self-taught, reading voluminously in libraries and spending a year at the University of California. In the late 1890s he joined the gold rush to the Klondike. This experience gave him material for his first book, 'The Son of Wolf', published in 1900, and for 'Call of the Wild' (1903), one of his most popular stories.

In his writing career of 17 years, London produced 50 books and many short stories. He wrote mostly for money, to meet ever-increasing expenses. His fame as a writer gave him a ready audience as a spokesman for a peculiar and inconsistent blend of socialism and racial superiority.

London's works, all hastily written, are of uneven quality. The best books are the Klondike tales, which also include 'White Fang' (1906) and 'Burning Daylight' (1910). His most enduring novel is probably the autobiographical 'Martin Eden' (1909), but the exciting 'Sea Wolf' (1904) continues to have great appeal for young readers.

In 1910 London settled near Glen Ellen, Calif., where he intended to build his dream home, "Wolf House." After the house burned down before completion in 1913, he was a broken and sick man. His death on Nov. 22, 1916, from an overdose of drugs, was probably a suicide.

--- Courtesy of Compton's Learning Company

INTRODUCTION

This unit has been designed to develop students' reading, writing, thinking, and language skills through exercises and activities related to *White Fang* by Jack London. It includes nineteen lessons, supported by extra resource materials.

The **introductory lesson** introduces students to the theme of domestication through an activity in which students show off pictures of their own pets and get some good information about caring for their pets from a representative of the SPCA. Following the introductory activity, students are given a transition to explain how the activity relates to the book they are about to read. Following the transition, students are given the materials they will be using during the unit. At the end of the lesson, students begin the pre-reading work for the first reading assignment.

The **reading assignments** are approximately thirty pages each; some are a little shorter while others are a little longer. Students have approximately 15 minutes of pre-reading work to do prior to each reading assignment. This pre-reading work involves reviewing the study questions for the assignment and doing some vocabulary work for 8 to 10 vocabulary words they will encounter in their reading.

The **study guide questions** are fact-based questions; students can find the answers to these questions right in the text. These questions come in two formats: short answer or multiple choice. The best use of these materials is probably to use the short answer version of the questions as study guides for students (since answers will be more complete), and to use the multiple choice for occasional quizzes. If your school has the appropriate equipment, it might be a good idea to make transparencies of your answer keys for the overhead projector.

The **vocabulary work** is intended to enrich students' vocabularies as well as to aid in the students' understanding of the book. Prior to each reading assignment, students will complete a two-part worksheet for approximately 8 to 10 vocabulary words in the upcoming reading assignment. Part I focuses on students' use of general knowledge and contextual clues by giving the sentence in which the word appears in the text. Students are then to write down what they think the words mean based on the words' usage. Part II nails down the definitions of the words by giving students dictionary definitions of the words and having students match the words to the correct definitions based on the words' contextual usage. Students should then have a thorough understanding of the words when they meet them in the text.

After each reading assignment, students will go back and formulate answers for the study guide questions. Discussion of these questions serves as a **review** of the most important events and ideas presented in the reading assignments.

After students complete reading the work, a lesson is devoted to the **extra discussion questions/writing assignments**. These questions focus on interpretation, critical analysis and personal response, employing a variety of thinking skills and adding to the students' understanding of the novel.

Following the discussion activity, there is a **vocabulary review** lesson which pulls together all of the fragmented vocabulary lists for the reading assignments and gives students a review of all of the words they have studied.

The vocabulary review is followed by a **project** which students may either complete independently or in small groups. Students research a suggested topic and then produce a persuasive advertisement related to that topic.

One class period is devoted to viewing the many advertisements the students have created; thus, the entire class is exposed to information about all of the topics.

There are three **writing assignments** in this unit, each with the purpose of informing, persuading, or having students express personal opinions. The first assignment is to give students the opportunity to express their personal opinions as they define the word "civilized." The second assignment is to inform: following the research related to their projects, students take the information they have found and summarize it in a composition. The third assignment is to persuade: students create a persuasive advertisement.

In addition, there is a **nonfiction reading assignment**. Students are required to read a piece of nonfiction related in some way to *White Fang*. After reading their nonfiction pieces, students will fill out a worksheet on which they answer questions regarding facts, interpretation, criticism, and personal opinions. In this unit, the nonfiction assignment is integrated into the students' project assignments.

The **review lesson** pulls together all of the aspects of the unit. The teacher is given four or five choices of activities or games to use which all serve the same basic function of reviewing all of the information presented in the unit.

The **unit test** comes in two formats: multiple choice or short answer. As a convenience, two different tests for each format have been included. There is also an advanced short answer test for higher level students.

There are additional **support materials** included with this unit. The **extra activities** section includes suggestions for an in-class library, crossword and word search puzzles related to the novel, and extra vocabulary worksheets. There is a list of **bulletin board ideas** which gives the teacher suggestions for bulletin boards to go along with this unit. In addition, there is a list of **extra class activities** the teacher could choose from to enhance the unit or as a substitution for an exercise the teacher might feel is inappropriate for his/her class. Materials for student use (worksheets, tests, etc. as well as any bulletin board graphics included in the unit) may be reproduced without infringement of the copyrights. No other portions of the literature unit plan may be reproduced without the written permission of Teacher's Pet Publications, Inc.

The **level** of this unit can be varied depending upon the criteria on which the individual assignments are graded, the teacher's expectations of his/her students in class discussions, and the formats chosen for the study guides, quizzes and test. If teachers have other ideas/activities they wish to use, they can usually easily be inserted prior to the review lesson.

UNIT OBJECTIVES - *White Fang*

1. Through reading London's *White Fang*, students will study the importance of adapting to the changes in one's life and environment.

2. Students will demonstrate their understanding of the text on four levels: factual, interpretive, critical and personal.

3. Students will discuss the role of animals in our world.

4. Students will discuss the merits and downfalls of human civilization.

5. Students will discuss the theme of survival of the fittest.

6. Students will be given the opportunity to practice reading aloud and silently to improve their skills in each area.

7. Students will answer questions to demonstrate their knowledge and understanding of the main events and characters in *White Fang* as they relate to the author's theme development.

8. Students will enrich their vocabularies and improve their understanding of the novel through the vocabulary lessons prepared for use in conjunction with the novel.

9. The writing assignments in this unit are geared to several purposes:
    a. To have students demonstrate their abilities to inform, to persuade, or to express their own personal ideas
        Note: Students will demonstrate ability to write effectively to <u>inform</u> by developing and organizing facts to convey information. Students will demonstrate the ability to write effectively to <u>persuade</u> by selecting and organizing relevant information, establishing an argumentative purpose, and by designing an appropriate strategy for an identified audience. Students will demonstrate the ability to write effectively to <u>express personal ideas</u> by selecting a form and its appropriate elements.
    b. To check the students' reading comprehension
    c. To make students think about the ideas presented by the novel
    d. To encourage logical thinking
    e. To provide an opportunity to practice good grammar and improve students' use of the English language.

READING ASSIGNMENT SHEET - *White Fang*

Date Assigned	Chapters Assigned	Completion Date
	I - III	
	IV - VII	
	VIII - XI	
	XII - XV	
	XVI - XIX	
	XX - XXII	
	XXIII - XXV	

UNIT OUTLINE - *White Fang*

1 Introduction PV 1-III	2 Read I-III	3 PVR IV-VII	4 Quiz/?s I-VII PVR VIII-XI	5 Study ?s VIII-XI Writing Assignment 1 PVR XII-XV
6 Study ?s XII-XV PVR XVI-XIX	7 Study ?s XVI-XIX PVR XX-XXII	8 Study ?s XX-XXII PVR XXIII-XV	9 Study ?s XXIII-XXV Extra ?s	10 Vocabulary
11 Writing Assignment 2	12 Project Assignments	13 Library	14 Planning Session	15 Production
16 Production	17 View Ads	18 Review	19 Test	

Key: P = Preview Study Questions   V = Prereading Vocabulary Work   R = Read

STUDY GUIDE QUESTIONS

SHORT ANSWER STUDY GUIDE QUESTIONS - *White Fang*

Chapters I-III
1. What was in the box?
2. Where does this story take place?
3. What animals were following Bill and Henry?
4. What happened to "Fatty"?
5. What other dog disappeared?
6. How did the she-wolf react to the gun?
7. To what did Bill compare the wolves?
8. How did the she-wolf fool One Ear?
9. What happened when Bill tried to save One Ear?
10. Why were the nights a terror?
11. How did Henry spend his days?
12. How was Henry saved?

Chapters IV-VII
1. For what was the wolf pack hunting?
2. About what were One Eye and the three year old fighting? Who won the battle?
3. How did the sapling scare One Eye?
4. For what was the she-wolf searching?
5. Why did the she-wolf growl at One Eye?
6. Why didn't One Eye just eat the ptarmigan?
7. How was one pup different from all the rest?
8. Why was the gray pup confused about the white wall?
9. What happened to One Eye?
10. What made the lynx especially vicious?
11. What did the gray cub find when he fell through the pine trunk?
12. How did the gray cub discover that he was carnivorous?
13. What about the water surprised the gray cub?
14. What happened to the mother weasel?

Chapters VIII-XI
1. What did the gray cub do to the young weasel?
2. What did the she-wolf give the gray cub to eat?
3. Why did the lynx fight with the she-wolf? Who won?
4. Why was the gray cub bolder after the fight with the lynx?
5. What did the gray cub see on the way to the stream?
6. Who is Kiche?
7. How did White Fang differentiate man from beast?
8. Why did the Indians laugh at White Fang?
9. Identify Lip-lip.
10. Why wouldn't Kiche go into the forest?

White Fang Short Answer Study Guide Page 2

11. What happened to White Fang when he followed his mother?
12. What was the "crime of crimes"?
13. What fighting technique did White Fang successfully use?
14. Describe White Fang at this point in the story.

Chapters XII-XV
1. How did White Fang get away from the Indians?
2. Identify Mit-sah.
3. Why did White Fang become afraid in the wild?
4. How did Gray Beaver react to White Fang's return?
5. Why did Mit-sah put Lip-lip at the head of the sled team?
6. Why was White Fang afraid of hands?
7. Why did the boy try to club White Fang? What was White Fang's response?
8. Why did White Fang defend Mit-sah?
9. Over what did Baseek and White Fang fight? Who won?
10. Why did Kiche slash White Fang's face?
11. Why did White Fang leave the Indian camp for a while?
12. What did White Fang get when he returned to the village?
13. What was the difference between White Fang and the other dogs?
14. What did White Fang think of the "white gods"?
15. How did White Fang escape punishment for killing the white men's dogs?

Chapters XVI-XIX
1. Who was Beauty Smith?
2. What did White Fang think of Beauty Smith?
3. Why did Gray Beaver sell White Fang?
4. What happened to White Fang when he returned to Gray Beaver?
5. For what did Beauty Smith use White Fang?
6. Why did White Fang always win his fights?
7. Identify Tim Keenan and Cherokee.
8. How was Cherokee different from the other dogs White Fang had fought?
9. When he knew the fight was lost, what did Beauty Smith do to White Fang?
10. Who saved White Fang?
11. Why did White Fang kill Major?
12. Why did White Fang bite Matt?
13. Why didn't Matt kill White Fang?

White Fang Short Answer Study Guide Page 3

Chapters XX-XXII
1. How did Weedon win White Fang's confidence?
2. What was White Fang's reaction to being a pet?
3. Why was Weedon Scott able to transform White Fang into a pet?
4. What did White Fang do when Weedon Scott left in the spring?
5. What was so important about White Fang's snuggling?
6. Who tried to steal White Fang? Why wasn't he successful?
7. Where was Weedon Scott going, and why did he decide to take White Fang?
8. How did White Fang feel about the city?
9. Why wouldn't White Fang fight the Collie?
10. Identify Dick.

Chapters XXIII-XXV
1. How did the Collie treat White Fang?
2. What did White Fang do to the groom?
3. What did Judge Scott have to do when White Fang didn't eat any chickens?
4. Why did White Fang kill the dogs at the crossroads?
5. Why did White Fang leave the injured Weedon Scott in the woods?
6. Why didn't White Fang go riding in the woods with his master in the fall?
7. Identify Jim Hall.
8. Why was Jim Hall angry with Judge Scott?
9. Who saved Judge Scott and at what cost?
10. What name did the women give White Fang?
11. How did the book end?

KEY: SHORT ANSWER STUDY GUIDE QUESTIONS - *White Fang*

<u>Chapters I-III</u>

1. What was in the box?
    A dead man was in the box.

2. Where does this story take place?
    It takes place in the far North.

3. What animals were following Bill and Henry?
    Wolves were following them.

4. What happened to "Fatty"?
    He was eaten by the wolves.

5. What other dog disappeared?
    Frog disappeared.

6. How did the she-wolf react to the gun?
    She dashed off into the trees; she seemed to know for what the gun would be used.

7. To what did Bill compare the wolves?
    He compared them to sharks.

8. How did the she-wolf fool One Ear?
    She pretended to be playful and then turned against him.

9. What happened when Bill tried to save One Ear?
    Both Bill and One Ear were eaten by the wolves.

10. Why were the nights a terror?
    The wolves were becoming bolder and coming closer to Henry as he slept.

11. How did Henry spend his days?
    He spent his days getting resupplied with firewood.

12. How was Henry saved?
    Some men with sleds were traveling by and happened to see him. They gave him transportation.

Chapters IV-VII

1. For what was the wolf pack hunting?
    The pack was hunting for herds of moose.

2. About what were One Eye and the three year old fighting? Who won the battle?
    They were fighting over the she-wolf. One Eye won the battle.

3. How did the sapling scare One Eye?
    There was a rabbit attached to the sapling. When One Eye pulled the rabbit, the sapling moved too, as if to hit him.

4. For what was the she-wolf searching?
    She was looking for a lair in which to have her pups.

5. Why did the she-wolf growl at One Eye?
    He had come too close to her and the pups.

6. Why didn't One Eye just eat the ptarmigan?
    He remembered he had a family at home depending on him for food.

7. How was one pup different from all the rest?
    One pup looked like his father; the rest looked like their mother.

8. Why was the gray pup confused about the white wall?
    He saw that his father could disappear into the white wall. Since he was not allowed to go near the white wall, he tried his father's trick on the other walls but only managed to get a sore nose. The white wall remained a mystery to him.

9. What happened to One Eye?
    He was killed by the lynx.

10. What made the lynx especially vicious?
    She had a litter of hungry kittens.

11. What did the gray cub find when he fell through the pine trunk?
    He discovered a nest of ptarmigan chicks.

12. How did the gray cub discover that he was carnivorous?
    He enjoyed eating the ptarmigan chicks.

13. What about the water surprised the gray cub?
    Even though it wasn't alive, it moved, and even though it appeared to be solid, it wasn't.

14. What happened to the mother weasel?
    She was killed by the she-wolf after she tried to eat the she-wolf's cub.

Chapters VIII-XI

1. What did the gray cub do to the young weasel?
    He killed and ate it.

2. What did the she-wolf give the gray cub to eat?
    She gave him a lynx kitten.

3. Why did the lynx fight with the she-wolf? Who won?
    The she-wolf had eaten her kittens. The she-wolf won.

4. Why was the gray cub bolder after the fight with the lynx?
    He had been in a fight with a larger animal and had survived.

5. What did the gray cub see on the way to the stream?
    He saw five Indians.

6. Who is Kiche?
    Kiche is the she-wolf. She was once an Indian dog (part-dog and part-wolf) who ran away to live with the wolves.

7. How did White Fang differentiate man from beast?
    Man didn't fight with fangs and claws; rather, he used "dead" things like clubs and guns.

8. Why did the Indians laugh at White Fang?
    He burned the tip of his nose and tongue.

9. Identify Lip-lip.
    Lip-lip was another dog who picked fights with White Fang in the Indian camp.

10. Why wouldn't Kiche go into the forest?
    She was still held by the bonds of man.

11. What happened to White Fang when he followed his mother?
    Gray Beaver followed him and gave him a severe beating.

12. What was the "crime of crimes"?
    Biting a man was absolutely forbidden.

13. What fighting technique did White Fang successfully use?
    He learned to use the element of surprise.

14. Describe White Fang at this point in the story.
   He has become vicious, cunning and very intelligent in the ways of war and survival among dogs.

Chapters XII-XV

1. How did White Fang get away from the Indians?
   He quietly sneaked out of the village in the midst of the confusion when the Indians were moving to a winter camp.

2. Identify Mit-sah.
   Mit-sah was Gray Beaver's son.

3. Why did White Fang become afraid in the wild?
   He had spent so much time in the care of men that he had forgotten what to do in the wild; life with men was much easier.

4. How did Gray Beaver react to White Fang's return?
   He gave White Fang a half of a piece of tallow.

5. Why did Mit-sah put Lip-lip at the head of the sled team?
   From the other dogs' point of view, Lip-lip would be running away from them; they would be chasing Lip-lip. By using the dogs' natural animosity towards Lip-lip, the sled would be pulled faster.

6. Why was White Fang afraid of hands?
   Hands controlled whips and clubs to hurt dogs.

7. Why did the boy try to club White Fang? What was White Fang's response?
   White Fang had eaten some frozen chips of moose meat which the boy was chopping. When the boy cornered him, White Fang bit the boy's club hand and fled to Gray Beaver.

8. Why did White Fang defend Mit-sah?
   Although the fight between the boys and Mit-sah was no concern of his, White Fang defended Mit-sah out of duty to his master.

9. Over what did Baseek and White Fang fight? Who won?
   The two dogs fought over a piece of moose meat that Baseek tried to take from White Fang. White Fang won the fight.

10. Why did Kiche slash White Fang's face?
    She didn't remember him; she saw him as an intruder.

11. Why did White Fang leave the Indian camp for a while?
>He left in search of food in the wild.

12. What did White Fang get when he returned to the village?
>Kloo-kooch gave him a whole, fresh-caught fish.

13. What was the difference between White Fang and the other dogs?
>The other dogs had been domesticated for several generations; White Fang had come directly from the wild.

14. What did White Fang think of the "white gods"?
>He felt that they were more powerful than the Indians.

15. How did White Fang escape punishment for killing the white men's dogs?
>He would pick a fight with a dog, overthrow it, and let the rest of the pack come in to finish it off. White Fang would then run away, leaving the pack to take the punishment for killing the dog.

Chapters XVI-XIX

1. Who was Beauty Smith?
>He was a mean, ugly man who delighted in White Fang's ferocious prowess.

2. What did White Fang think of Beauty Smith?
>He hated Beauty with all of his heart.

3. Why did Gray Beaver sell White Fang?
>He had become an alcoholic and sold White Fang for some bottles of whiskey.

4. What happened to White Fang when he returned to Gray Beaver?
>Gray Beaver tied him up and returned him to Beauty Smith.

5. For what did Beauty Smith use White Fang?
>He used him as a fighting dog. He tormented White Fang to keep him in a constant rage so people who would come to see him fight would get their money's worth.

6. Why did White Fang always win his fights?
>He won because he was born wild and had in all his life become skilled and experienced at fighting.

7. Identify Tim Keenan and Cherokee.
>He brought a bulldog named Cherokee to fight White Fang.

8. How was Cherokee different from the other dogs White Fang had fought?
    He was short and soft and had short hair.

9. When he knew the fight was lost, what did Beauty Smith do to White Fang?
    He kicked him.

10. Who saved White Fang?
    Weedon Scott saved him.

11. Why did White Fang kill Major?
    He killed Major because Major tried to take his meat.

12. Why did White Fang bite Matt?
    He bit Matt because Matt kicked him for killing Major.

13. Why didn't Matt kill White Fang?
    Every time he put the rifle to his shoulder, White Fang would growl and bristle. When he put the rifle down, White Fang would respond by becoming calmer. Matt and Weedon Scott realized that White Fang was too smart to kill.

Chapters XX-XXII

1. How did Weedon win White Fang's confidence?
    He spoke softly to him and fed him good meat.

2. What was White Fang's reaction to being a pet?
    He was afraid that the "god" would at any minute hit him with the hands that were presently petting him.

3. Why was Weedon Scott able to transform White Fang into a pet?
    He was a compassionate, understanding, loving person.

4. What did White Fang do when Weedon Scott left in the spring?
    He would not eat and became very weak and sick.

5. What was so important about White Fang's snuggling?
    He was saying, "You have my total confidence." This, from a dog who had formerly been vicious.

6. Who tried to steal White Fang? Why wasn't he successful?
    Beauty Smith tried to steal White Fang, but White Fang attacked him (and probably would have killed him had Weedon Scott not intervened).

7. Where was Weedon Scott going, and why did he decide to take White Fang?
    He was going to California. He decided to take White Fang with him because he knew that White Fang would starve himself to death if he could not go with his master. The final decision came when White Fang jumped through glass to be with his master.

8. How did White Fang feel about the city?
    He hated it. It was too confusing and frightening, and it made him feel small.

9. Why wouldn't White Fang fight the Collie?
    The Collie was a female, and his instincts told him never to fight with a female.

10. Identify Dick.
    Dick was a deerhound who belonged to Judge Scott.

Chapters XXIII-XXV
1. How did the Collie treat White Fang?
    She picked on him.

2. What did White Fang do to the groom?
    He ripped open the groom's arm.

3. What did Judge Scott have to do when White Fang didn't eat any chickens?
    He had to repeatedly say, "White Fang, you are smarter than I thought."

4. Why did White Fang kill the dogs at the crossroads?
    The dogs at the crossroads always taunted White Fang who would never fight back because his master had told him not to fight. One day the owners of the dogs sicced them onto White Fang, whose owner gave him permission to fight. So, White Fang fought them and killed them.

5. Why did White Fang leave the injured Weedon Scott in the woods?
    Weedon told White Fang to go home, which he did. When he got there, he let it be known that his master needed help.

6. Why didn't White Fang go riding in the woods with his master in the fall?
    He and the Collie had made friends, so he went off with her instead of his master.

7. Identify Jim Hall.
    He was an escaped prisoner, a mad-man who behaved like a jungle animal. He attempted to kill Judge Scott.

8. Why was Jim Hall angry with Judge Scott?
    Jim Hall did not commit the crime for which he was punished. He believed Judge Scott took part in the evidence cover-up with the police.

9. Who saved Judge Scott and at what cost?
    White Fang saved the judge but received three broken ribs and a gunshot wound.

10. What name did the women give White Fang?
    They called him "Blessed Wolf."

11. How did the book end?
    White Fang was alive and well with his puppies around him in the sunlight.

MULTIPLE CHOICE STUDY GUIDE/QUIZ QUESTIONS - *White Fang*

<u>Chapters I-III</u>

1. What was in the box?
    a. Supplies
    b. Dead man
    c. Lumber
    d. Household goods

2. Where does this story take place?
    a. In the far North
    b. In Greenland
    c. In Iceland
    d. In Russia

3. What animals were following Bill and Henry?
    a. Caribou
    b. Moose
    c. Wolves
    d. Bears

4. What happened to "Fatty"?
    a. He fell through thin ice.
    b. He was eaten by wolves.
    c. He starved to death.
    d. The other dogs attacked him.

5. How did the she-wolf react to the gun?
    a. Crouched low to the ground
    b. Began to howl
    c. Just stood and looked at it
    d. Dashed off into the trees

6. To what did Bill compare the wolves?
    a. Sharks
    b. Thieves
    c. Men
    d. Women

White Fang Multiple Choice Study Guide Page 2

7. How did the she-wolf fool One Ear?
    a. Crouched low and hid in the bushes
    b. Snatched the rabbit before One Ear could get it
    c. Pretended to be playful then turned against him
    d. Walked in the sled tracks

8. What happened when Bill tried to save One Ear?
    a. Bill barely managed to save One Ear.
    b. One Ear turned on him.
    c. Both Bill and One Ear were eaten.
    d. One Ear saved them both.

9. Why were the nights a terror?
    a. The wolves were becoming bolder and coming closer.
    b. Henry worried about the wolves and the Indians.
    c. Henry had no fire and was afraid of freezing to death.
    d. There were many strange sounds in the wilderness.

10. How did Henry spend his days?
    a. Caring for Bill
    b. Looking for food
    c. Fighting wolves
    d. Gathering firewood

11. How was Henry saved?
    a. He reached a village.
    b. Men with sleds happened to find him.
    c. The wolves mysteriously disappeared.
    d. The wolves gave up and went elsewhere to find food.

White Fang Multiple Choice Study Guide Page 3

Chapters IV-VII

1. For what was the wolf pack hunting?
    a. Henry
    b. The She-wolf
    c. Moose
    d. Rabbits

2. Over what were One Eye and the three year old fighting?
    a. The right to lead the pack
    b. The sack that fell off of the sled
    c. Meat
    d. The she-wolf

3. For what was the she-wolf searching?
    a. Food
    b. A place to have her pups
    c. One-Eye
    d. Water

4. Why did the she-wolf growl at One Eye?
    a. He had come too close to her and the pups
    b. He had tried to take more than his share of the meat
    c. It was a growl of affection
    d. She wanted him to go find food

5. Why didn't One Eye just eat the ptarmigan?
    a. The bird got away
    b. He remember he had a family to feed
    c. He had grown to like the little bird
    d. He was curious about it

6. How was one pup different from all the rest?
    a. It was a runt
    b. It was huge
    c. It was spotted
    d. It looked like its father

White Fang Multiple Choice Study Guide Page 4

7. What confused the gray pup?
    a. The white wall
    b. The floor
    c. The snow
    d. The lynx

8. What happened to One Eye?
    a. The she-wolf got mad and killed him.
    b. The lynx killed him.
    c. He went away as was the custom of the male wolves.
    d. Hunters killed him.

9. What made the lynx especially vicious?
    a. She was pregnant.
    b. She was ill.
    c. She had a litter of hungry kittens.
    d. She was wounded.

10. What did the gray cub find when he fell through the pine trunk?
    a. Lynx cubs
    b. One Eye
    c. Mother lynx
    d. Ptarmigan chicks

11. How did the gray cub discover that he was carnivorous?
    a. He enjoyed eating one of the cubs.
    b. He licked the wound he got from his fall, tasted blood and like it.
    c. He enjoyed eating the chicks.
    d. He enjoyed eating the meat his mother brought.

12. What happened to the mother weasel?
    a. The She-Wolf killed it.
    b. The gray cub killed it.
    c. One-Eye killed it.
    d. The lynx killed it.

White Fang Multiple Choice Study Guide Page 5

<u>Chapters VIII-XI</u>

1. What did the gray cub do to the young weasel?
    a. Played with it
    b. Wounded it and watched it run off
    c. Took it for his mother to look at it
    d. Killed and ate it

2. What did the she-wolf give the gray cub to eat?
    a. The young weasel
    b. A lynx kitten
    c. A ptarmigan chick
    d. Meat from mother lynx

3. Why was the gray cub bolder after the fight with the lynx?
    a. He was determined to do better the next time.
    b. He was stronger after a good meal.
    c. He had been in a fight with a larger animal and had survived.
    d. He was too tired to be cautious.

4. What did the gray cub see on the way to the stream?
    a. Mother lynx
    b. The carcass of his dead father
    c. Indians
    d. His mother

5. Who is Kiche?
    a. The she-wolf
    b. The Indian who used to own the she-wolf
    c. The gray cub's brother
    d. The she-wolf's new owner

6. How did White Fang differentiate man from beast?
    a. Man walked on his hind legs.
    b. Man had fire.
    c. Man smelled different.
    d. Man fought with clubs and guns.

White Fang Multiple Choice Study Guide Page 6

7. Why did the Indians laugh at White Fang?
    a. He wouldn't eat.
    b. He burned the tip of his nose.
    c. He was covered with mud.
    d. He ran into a wall.

8. Identify Lip-lip.
    a. White Fang's new dog friend
    b. Kiche's sister
    c. An Indian dog that picked on White Fang
    d. White Fang's new owner

9. Why wouldn't Kiche go into the forest?
    a. She was chained to a tree.
    b. She wanted to stay with White Fang.
    c. She was frightened.
    d. She wanted to stay with people.

10. What happened to White Fang when he followed his mother?
    a. He got lost.
    b. The She-Wolf nipped him.
    c. Gray Beaver beat him.
    d. Kiche called him back.

11. What was the "crime of crimes"?
    a. Leaving man
    b. Biting man
    c. Disobeying man
    d. Stealing from man

12. What fighting technique did White Fang successfully use?
    a. Surprise
    b. Feigning
    c. Holding the throat
    d. Clawing

13. Describe White Fang at this point in the story.
    a. Vicious, cunning and intelligent
    b. Wise and timid
    c. Smart but naive
    d. Lonely but brave

White Fang Multiple Choice Study Guide Page 7

<u>Chapters XII-XV</u>

1. How did White Fang get away from the Indians?
    a. He got away from Gray Beaver when they were out alone.
    b. He sneaked out in the middle of the night.
    c. He became so violent the Indians let him go.
    d. He sneaked away during the confusion of moving.

2. Identify Mit-sah.
    a. White Fang's new owner
    b. Another dog in the Indian camp
    c. Gray Beaver's son
    d. Gray Beaver's wife

3. Why did White Fang return to Gray Beaver?
    a. Gray Beaver came after him and forced him to return.
    b. Life with man was much easier than life in the wild.
    c. He couldn't find his mother.
    d. He was wounded.

4. How did Gray Beaver react to White Fang's return?
    a. Gray Beaver beat White Fang.
    b. Gray Beaver chained him to a tree.
    c. Gray Beaver locked him up.
    d. Gray Beaver game him a piece of tallow.

5. Why did Mit-sah put Lip-lip at the head of the sled team?
    a. Lip-Lip was the best sled dog.
    b. He was using the dogs' natural animosity.
    c. That's the only place Lip-lip would accept.
    d. Lip-lip had earned it.

6. Why was White Fang afraid of hands?
    a. They looked strange.
    b. They were always moving.
    c. They often held clubs and whips.
    d. He didn't understand them.

White Fang Multiple Choice Study Guide Page 8

7. Why did White Fang bite the boy?
    a. The boy cornered him.
    b. The boy beat him.
    c. He was afraid of the boy's hands.
    d. He wanted the boy's meat.

8. Why did White Fang defend Mit-sah?
    a. White Fang didn't like the other boy.
    b. The other boy was teasing White Fang, too.
    c. The other boy had hit White Fang by mistake.
    d. He did it out of duty to his master.

9. Over what did Baseek and White Fang fight?
    a. Mit-sah
    b. Moose meat
    c. Gray Beaver
    d. Territorial position

10. Why did Kiche slash White Fang's face?
    a. She was trying to teach him a lesson.
    b. It was an accident.
    c. She didn't recognize him.
    d. She wanted him to return to Gray Beaver.

11. Why did White Fang leave the Indian camp for a while?
    a. To look for food
    b. To look for his mother again
    c. To look for Gray Beaver
    d. To look for Mit-sah

12. What did White Fang get when he returned to the village?
    a. A beating
    b. A new master
    c. A whole fish
    d. A piece of tallow

13. What was the difference between White Fang and the other dogs?
    a. White Fang was more timid
    b. White Fang was older
    c. The other dogs were domesticated
    d. The other dogs were wiser

White Fang Multiple Choice Study Guide Page 9

14. What did White Fang think of the "white gods"?
    a. He liked them.
    b. The thought they were not very smart.
    c. He trusted them.
    d. They were more powerful than the Indians.

15. How did White Fang escape punishment for killing the white men's dogs?
    a. He was so vicious the men didn't want to bother with him
    b. He made it look like the other dogs in the pack did it
    c. He killed the dogs at night
    d. He made it look like the wild wolves did it

White Fang Multiple Choice Study Guide Page 10

Chapters XVI-XIX

1. Who was Beauty Smith?
    a. He was a scar-faced Indian who befriended White Fang.
    b. He was a handsome man of about 40 who bought White Fang.
    c. He was a mean, ugly man who delighted in White Fang's ferocious prowess.
    d. He was an ugly man who was determined to tame White Fang.

2. What did White Fang think of Beauty Smith?
    a. White Fang admired him.
    b. White Fang feared him.
    c. White Fang hated him.
    d. White Fang loved him.

3. Why did Gray Beaver sell White Fang?
    a. He wanted whiskey.
    b. He was tired of retrieving White Fang from the wild.
    c. He decided to move away and couldn't take White Fang with him.
    d. White Fang was nothing but trouble for him.

4. What happened to White Fang when he returned to Gray Beaver?
    a. He found Gray Beaver was gone.
    b. Gray Beaver took him back to Beauty Smith.
    c. Gray Beaver beat him severely.
    d. Kloo-kooch gave him a hearty meal.

5. For what did Beauty Smith use White Fang?
    a. Sled dog
    b. Pet
    c. Work dog
    d. Fighting dog

6. Why did White Fang always win his fights?
    a. He fought only smaller, domesticated dogs.
    b. Beauty wouldn't take a fight he didn't know White Fang could win.
    c. The experiences of his life had made him a skillful fighter.
    d. The fights were "fixed."

White Fang Multiple Choice Study Guide Page 11

7. Identify Cherokee.
    a. A bulldog brought to fight White Fang
    b. An Indian dog brought to fight White Fang
    c. He brought a bull dog to fight White Fang
    d. Beauty Smith's friend

8. How was Cherokee different from the other dogs White Fang had fought?
    a. He was a more experienced fighter and had more spirit.
    b. He was born wild.
    c. He was bigger.
    d. He was short and soft and had short hair.

9. When he knew the fight was lost, what did Beauty Smith do to White Fang?
    a. He shot him.
    b. He kicked him.
    c. He quickly sold him.
    d. He pulled him out of the fighting area, paid his debts and left.

10. Who saved White Fang?
    a. Cherokee
    b. Matt
    c. Weedon Scott
    d. Major

11. Why did White Fang kill Major?
    a. Major tried to take his meat.
    b. Major was his opponent.
    c. Major attacked him.
    d. White Fang was in a killing frenzy after the fight.

12. Why did White Fang bite Matt?
    a. Matt tried to take his meat.
    b. Matt kicked him for killing Major.
    c. Matt cornered him.
    d. Matt was shooting at him.

13. Why didn't Matt kill White Fang?
    a. He missed; White Fang got away.
    b. He was out of ammunition.
    c. He realized White Fang was too smart to kill.
    d. He didn't have the nerve.

White Fang Multiple Choice Study Guide Page 12

<u>Chapters XX-XXII</u>

1. How did Weedon win White Fang's confidence?
    a. He left him alone for several months, only feeding him.
    b. He made White Fang feel useful by giving him jobs.
    c. He saved White Fang's life.
    d. He spoke softly to White Fang and gave him good meat.

2. What was White Fang's reaction to being a pet?
    a. He loved it!
    b. He was still afraid of man's hands.
    c. He just wanted to escape back to the wild.
    d. He was too vicious to be tamed.

3. Why was Weedon Scott able to transform White Fang into a pet?
    a. He genuinely cared for White Fang and White Fang gradually learned that.
    b. He was a master at animal psychology.
    c. He was a forceful relentless master who wouldn't take no for an answer.
    d. He followed the advice he was given.

4. What did White Fang do when Weedon Scott left in the spring?
    a. He went to look for his master.
    b. He would not eat and became sick.
    c. He carried on "as usual."
    d. He ran away back to the wild.

5. What was so important about White Fang's snuggling?
    a. It kept Weedon Smith warm.
    b. It helped him get well.
    c. It showed his total confidence in Weedon Scott.
    d. It was his way of saying he was lonely.

6. Who tried to steal White Fang?
    a. Beauty Smith
    b. Matt
    c. Weedon Scott
    d. Cherokee

White Fang Multiple Choice Study Guide Page 13

7. Why did Weedon Scott decide to take White Fang with him?
    a. He needed a guard dog.
    b. He needed a sled dog.
    c. He realized White Fang would die without him.
    d. He wanted to take White Fang as a present to his father.

8. How did White Fang feel about the city?
    a. He loved it.
    b. He hated it.
    c. He didn't like it, but it was interesting.
    d. He liked it but preferred the wilderness.

9. Why wouldn't White Fang fight the Collie?
    a. His fighting days were over.
    b. He didn't want to kill the Judge's dog.
    c. He was afraid of her.
    d. His instincts would not let him fight a female.

10. Identify Dick.
    a. Judge Scott's deerhound
    b. Judge Scott's servant
    c. Judge Scott's gardener
    d. Weedon Scott's friend

White Fang Multiple Choice Study Guide Page 14

Chapters XXIII-XXV

1. How did the Collie treat White Fang?
    a. She feared him.
    b. She picked on him.
    c. She admired him.
    d. She ignored him.

2. What did White Fang do to the groom?
    a. Killed him
    b. Licked him
    c. Ripped open his arm
    d. Saved him

3. What did Judge Scott have to do when White Fang didn't eat any chickens?
    a. He had to repeatedly say, "White Fang you are smarter than I thought."
    b. He had to buy White Fang a new kennel.
    c. He had to let White Fang live inside the house.
    d. He had to apologize to Weedon.

4. Why did White Fang kill the dogs at the crossroads?
    a. They took his food.
    b. They attacked the Judge.
    c. The dogs attacked the collie.
    d. The dogs had taunted White Fang, and given permission to fight.

5. Why did White Fang leave the injured Weedon Scott in the woods?
    a. He went to chase a rabbit.
    b. His master told him to go.
    c. He didn't realize his master was injured.
    d. He got confused.

6. Why didn't White Fang go riding in the woods with his master in the fall?
    a. He was ill.
    b. Weedon Scott told him to stay home.
    c. The woods brought back bad memories.
    d. He preferred the company of the Collie.

White Fang Multiple Choice Study Guide Page 15

7. Identify Jim Hall.
    a. He was a friend of the judge.
    b. He tried to kill the judge.
    c. He was White Fang's new master.
    d. He was Beauty Smith's friend.

8. Why was Jim Hall angry with Judge Scott?
    a. The judge cheated him.
    b. He thought the judge jailed him unjustly.
    c. The judge wouldn't "play ball" politically.
    d. The judge snubbed him.

9. Who saved Judge Scott and at what cost?
    a. Weedon Scott
    b. Jim Hall
    c. White Fang
    d. Collie

10. What name did the women give White Fang?
    a. Rin-Tin-tin
    b. Brave Wolf
    c. Wolf-dog
    d. Blessed Wolf

11. What happened to White Fang?
    a. He lived happily ever after with the Scotts and the Collie.
    b. He died from wounds he got while saving the judge.
    c. He eventually returned to the wild.
    d. He was put to sleep.

KEY: MULTIPLE CHOICE STUDY QUESTIONS - *White Fang*

I-III	IV-VII	VIII-XI	XII-XV
1. B	1. C	1. D	1. D
2. A	2. D	2. B	2. C
3. C	3. B	3. C	3. B
4. B	4. A	4. C	4. D
5. D	5. B	5. A	5. B
6. A	6. D	6. D	6. C
7. C	7. A	7. B	7. A
8. C	8. B	8. C	8. D
9. A	9. C	9. D	9. B
10. D	10. D	10. C	10. C
11. B	11. C	11. B	11. A
	12. A	12. A	12. C
		13. A	13. C
			14. D
			15. B

XVI - XIX	XX-XXII	XXIII-XXV
1. C	1. D	1. B
2. C	2. B	2. C
3. A	3. A	3. A
4. B	4. B	4. D
5. D	5. C	5. B
6. C	6. B	6. D
7. A	7. C	7. B
8. D	8. B	8. B
9. B	9. D	9. C
10. C	10. A	10. D
11. A		11. A
12. B		
13. C		

PREREADING VOCABULARY WORKSHEETS

Vocabulary - *White Fang*

<u>Chapters 1-3</u> Part I: Using Prior Knowledge and Contextual Clues

Below are the sentences in which the vocabulary words appear in the text. Read the sentence. Use any clues you can find in the sentence combined with your prior knowledge, and write what you think the underlined words mean on the lines provided.

1. But there was life, abroad in the land and <u>defiant</u>.

___

2. Who is the most restless of life, ever in revolt against the <u>dictum</u> that all movement must in the end come to the cessation of movement.

___

3. It soared upward with a swift rush, till it reached its topmost note, where is persisted, <u>palpitant</u> and tense.

___

4. Henry was aroused by fervid <u>blasphemy</u> that proceeded from the mouth of Bill.

___

5. A flush of angry blood <u>pervaded</u> Bill's face.

___

6. The day began <u>auspiciously</u>.

___

7. She seemed to smile at him, showing her teeth in an <u>ingratiating</u> rather than a menacing way.

___

8. But whatever idea was forming in his mind, was <u>dissipated</u> by the she-wolf, who advanced upon him.

___

9. The snarling of his dogs was losing its <u>efficacy</u>.

___

White Fang Vocabulary for Chapters 1-3 Continued

Part II: Determining the Meaning - Match the vocabulary words to their dictionary definitions. If there are words for which you cannot figure out the definition by contextual clues and by process of elimination, look them up in a dictionary.

___ 1. Defiant	A. swearing, speaking irreverently
___ 2. Dictum	B. favorably
___ 3. Palpitant	C. vanished, scattered
___ 4. Blasphemy	D. willing to provoke
___ 5. Pervaded	E. force, energy
___ 6. Auspiciously	F. an authoritative saying, ruling
___ 7. Ingratiating	G. permeated, flowed through
___ 8. Dissipated	H. trembling, throbbing
___ 9. Efficacy	I. trying to get into another's good will

Vocabulary - *White Fang* Chapters 4-7

Part I: Using Prior Knowledge and Contextual Clues

    Below are the sentences in which the vocabulary words appear in the text. Read the sentence. Use any clues you can find in the sentence combined with your prior knowledge, and write what you think the underlined words mean on the lines provided.

1. He merely sprang to the side and ran stiffly ahead for several awkward leaps, in carriage and conduct resembling an <u>abashed</u> country swain.

   _____

2. But if they could fast <u>prodigiously</u> they could feed prodigiously, and soon a few scattered bones were all that remained.

   _____

3. Slowly, cautiously, it was unrolling its ball of <u>impregnable</u> armor.

   _____

4. It had been ripped almost in half, and was till bleeding <u>profusely</u>.

   _____

5. He was never <u>oppressed</u> by the narrow confines of his existence.

   _____

6. Growth had assumed the <u>guise</u> of curiosity.

   _____

7. When a moosebird <u>impudently</u> hopped up to him, he reached out at it with a playful paw.

   _____

8. He blundered upon meat just outside his own cave door on his first <u>foray</u> into the world.

   _____

9. It was the sum of the terrors of the unknown, the one <u>culminating</u> and unthinkable catastrophe that could happen to him.

   _____

White Fang Vocabulary for Chapters 4-7 Continued

Part II: Determining the Meaning - Match the vocabulary words to their dictionary definitions.

___ 10. Abashed
___ 11. Prodigiously
___ 12. Impregnable
___ 13. Profusely
___ 14. Oppressed
___ 15. Guise
___ 16. Impudently
___ 17. Foray
___ 18. Culminating

A. behavior
B. forward in behavior, bold-faced
C. reaching the highest point
D. lavishly, exuberantly
E. predatory excursion
F. ashamed
G. overpowered, overburdened
H. extraordinarily, enormously in the past
I. able to resist attack, invincible

Vocabulary - *White Fang* Chapters 8-10

Part I: Using Prior Knowledge and Contextual Clues

Below are the sentences in which the vocabulary words appear in the text. Read the sentence. Use any clues you can find in the sentence combined with your prior knowledge, and write what you think the underlined words mean on the lines provided.

1. Assured of his own intrepidity, he abandoned himself to petty rages and lusts.

___

2. He might have epitomized life as a voracious appetite.

___

3. There were a myriad other and lesser laws for him to learn and obey.

___

4. Even the bridge of the nose wrinkling from tip to eyes so prodigious was her snarl.

___

5. A part-grown puppy, somewhat larger and older than he, came toward him slowly, with ostentatious and belligerent importance.

___

6. It impinged on his nerves and senses, made him nervous and restless and worried him.

___

7. The more he came to know them, the more they vindicated their superiority, the more they displayed their mysterious power.

___

8. Successfully to devise ways and means of avoiding his implacable persecutor.

___

9. Impelled by the blows that rained upon him ... White Fang swung back and forth like an erratic and jerky pendulum.

___

White Fang Vocabulary for Chapters 8-10 Continued

Part II: Determining the Meaning - Match the vocabulary words to their dictionary definitions.

___ 19. Intrepidity
___ 20. Epitomized
___ 21. Myriad
___ 22. Prodigious
___ 23. Ostentatious
___ 24. Impinged
___ 25. Vindicated
___ 26. Implacable
___ 27. Impelled

A. proved to be just or valid
B. driven or urged forward, pressed upon
C. vain, pomp, ambitious display
D. unrelenting, cannot be appeased
E. a countless number, innumerable
F. huge, enormous
G. fearless, bold
H. clashed, dashed against
I. summarized, condensed

Vocabulary - *White Fang* Chapters 11-15

Part I: Using Prior Knowledge and Contextual Clues

Below are the sentences in which the vocabulary words appear in the text. Read the sentence. Use any clues you can find in the sentence combined with your prior knowledge, and write what you think the underlined words mean on the lines provided.

1. Perhaps they sensed his wild-wood breed, and instinctively felt for him, the <u>enmity</u> that the domestic dog feels for the wolf.

_____

2. His <u>sanguinary</u> methods and remarkable efficiency made the pack pay for its persecution of him.

_____

3. Where the river swung in against <u>precipitous</u> bluffs, he climbed the high mountains behind.

_____

4. But he knew, further, that the comfort of the fire would be his, the protection of the gods, the companionship of the dogs-the last, a companionship of enmity, but none the less a companionship and satisfying to his <u>gregarious</u> needs.

_____

5. White Fang crawled slowly, cringing and groveling in the abjectness of his <u>abasement</u> and submission.

_____

6. When they came near with their <u>ominous</u> hands, he got up.

_____

7. Not only was such an act <u>sacrilegious</u> in its nature, but it was fraught with peril.

_____

8. Had there been in White Fang's nature any possibility, ... of his ever coming to <u>fraternize</u> with his kind, such possibility was irretrievably destroyed when he was made leader of the sled team.

_____

9. His feet clung to the earth with the same <u>tenacity</u> that he clung to life.

_____

White Fang Vocabulary for Chapters 11-15 Continued

Part II: Determining the Meaning - Match the vocabulary words to their dictionary definitions.

___ 28. Enmity   A. toughness
___ 29. Sanguinary   B. living in a pack, not solitary
___ 30. Precipitous   C. hostility, opposition
___ 31. Gregarious   D. confident
___ 32. Abasement   E. violation of something sacred
___ 33. Ominous   F. to associate with
___ 34. Sacrilegious   G. disgraced
___ 35. Fraternize   H. an ill omen
___ 36. Tenacity   I. very steep

Vocabulary - *White Fang* Chapters 16-19

Part I: Using Prior Knowledge and Contextual Clues

Below are the sentences in which the vocabulary words appear in the text. Read the sentence. Use any clues you can find in the sentence combined with your prior knowledge, and write what you think the underlined words mean on the lines provided.

1. He had a sharp and covetous eye for White Fang.

_____

2. It slanted uncompromisingly to meet a low and remarkably wide forehead.

_____

3. He owed no allegiance to this strange and terrible god.

_____

4. Under the tutelage of the mad god, White Fang became a fiend.

_____

5. He was too ponderous and slow.

_____

6. He would be dragging around in the whirl of one of White Fang's mad gyrations.

_____

7. He struggled vainly to shake off the clinging death.

_____

8. Besides, there was his old antipathy to being touched.

_____

White Fang Vocabulary for Chapters 16-19 Continued

Part II: Determining the Meaning
    Match the vocabulary words to their dictionary definitions. If there are words for which you cannot figure out the definition by contextual clues and by process of elimination, look them up in a dictionary.

___ 37. Covetous   A. futile, pointless
___ 38. Tutelage   B. sporadic movements
___ 39. Uncompromisingly   C. under the guardianship of
___ 40. Allegiance   D. dislike, opposition
___ 41. Ponderous   E. rigid, strict, unyielding
___ 42. Gyrations   F. massive and awkward
___ 43. Vainly   G. loyalty
___ 44. Antipathy   H. be desirable of, longing for unlawfully

Vocabulary - *White Fang* Chapters 20-22

Part I: Using Prior Knowledge and Contextual Clues

Below are the sentences in which the vocabulary words appear in the text. Read the sentence. Use any clues you can find in the sentence combined with your prior knowledge, and write what you think the underlined words mean.

1. But the god talked on interminably.

___

2. There was no telling when the god's ulterior motive might be disclosed.

___

3. But the man who sent softly, by circuitous ways, peering with caution, seeking after secrecy-that was the man who received no suspension of judgment from White Fang.

___

4. There was a burgeoning within him of strange feelings and unwonted impulses.

___

5. Too long had he cultivated reticence, aloofness, and moroseness.

___

6. His master rarely fed him; Matt did that, it was his business; yet White Fang divined that it was his master's food he ate and that it was his master who thus fed him vicariously.

___

7. That White Fang should quickly gain the post was inevitable.

___

8. Life was flowing through him again, splendid and indomitable.

___

9. The thunder of the streets smote upon his ears.

___

White Fang Vocabulary for Chapters 20-22 Continued

Part II: Determining the Meaning - Match the vocabulary words to their dictionary definitions.

___ 45. Interminably
___ 46. Ulterior
___ 47. Circuitous
___ 48. Burgeoning
___ 49. Reticence
___ 50. Vicariously
___ 51. Inevitable
___ 52. Indomitable
___ 53. Smote

A. bound to happen
B. irrepressible, invincible
C. reserve; restraint
D. attacked, damaged or destroyed by or as if by blows
E. roundabout; indirect
F. undisclosed; hidden
G. blossoming; growing
H. fulfilled by the substitution of another person or thing
I. endlessly

Vocabulary - *White Fang* Chapters 23-25

Part I: Using Prior Knowledge and Contextual Clues
　　Below are the sentences in which the vocabulary words appear in the text. Read the sentence. Use any clues you can find in the sentence combined with your prior knowledge, and write what you think the underlined words mean on the lines provided.

1. Had Dick had his way, they would have been good friends; but White Fang was adverse to friendship.

   _____

2. They cooked for the master and washed the dishes and did other things, just as Matt had done in the Klondike. They were, in short appurtenances.

   _____

3. But Collie did not give over as was her wont, after a decent interval of chastisement. On the contrary she grew more excited and angry every moment.

   _____

4. But it was the multiplicity of laws that befuddled White Fang.

   _____

5. But there is a certain sense of equity that resides in life, and it was this sense in him that resented the unfairness of his being permitted no defense against the stone-throwers.

   _____

6. His naked fangs, and writhing lips were uniformly efficacious, rarely failing to send a bellowing onrushing dog back on its haunches.

   _____

7. In San Quentin prison he had proved incorrigible. Punishment failed to break his spirit.

   _____

8. The surgeon smiled indulgently. "Of course, I understand.

   _____

9. Down out of the blue it would rush, as it dropped upon him changing itself into the ubiquitous electric car.

   _____

White Fang Vocabulary for Chapters 23-25 Continued

Part II: Determining the Meaning - Match the vocabulary words to their dictionary definitions.

___ 54. Adverse
___ 55. Appurtenances
___ 56. Chastisement
___ 57. Befuddled
___ 58. Equity
___ 59. Incorrigible
___ 60. Indulgently
___ 61. Ubiquitous
___ 62. Efficacious

A. baffled; puzzled
B. ever present
C. opposed to; against
D. admonishment, rebuking, reprimanding
E. appendages
F. fairness
G. unmanageable
H. obligingly; tolerantly
I. capable of producing the desired effect

VOCABULARY ANSWER KEY
White Fang

Chapters 1-3	Chapters 4-7	Chapters 8-10	Chapters 11-15
1. D	10. F	19. G	28. C
2. F	11. H	20. I	29. D
3. H	12. I	21. E	30. I
4. A	13. D	22. F	31. B
5. G	14. G	23. C	32. G
6. B	15. A	24. H	33. H
7. I	16. B	25. A	34. E
8. C	17. E	26. D	35. F
9. E	18. C	27. B	36. A

Chapters 16-19	Chapters 20-22	Chapters 23-25
37. H	45. I	54. C
38. C	46. F	55. E
39. E	47. E	56. D
40. G	48. G	57. A
41. F	49. C	58. F
42. B	50. H	59. G
43. A	51. A	60. H
44. D	52. B	61. B
	53. D	62. I

DAILY LESSONS

LESSON ONE

Objectives
    1. To introduce the *White Fang* unit.
    2. To distribute books and other related materials (study guides, reading assignments, etc.).
    3. To preview the study questions for chapters I-III
    4. To familiarize students with the vocabulary for chapters I-III

NOTE: Prior to this lesson, you need to have made the assignment for your students to bring in pictures of their pets (or pictures of animals they wish were their pets if they have none.) Also, you need to have put up background paper on your bulletin board and a title: DOMESTICATED ANIMALS.

Activity #1
    Ask your students to take the pictures of their pets out. Tell them to take the pictures of their pets to the bulletin board, pin them up, and write the pets' names under the pictures. After students have done this, take a few minutes to look at the pets and make some comments about them. ("Crackers? Who has a dog named Crackers? How did he get that name?, etc.)

Activity #2
    Transition: "I see many of you do have pets, so you will probably be interested in listening to the guest I have invited to talk with you today."
    Introduce your guest, a representative from your local SPCA or humane society, who will talk to your students about proper care for pets of all kinds. Perhaps the representative could bring a live pet along to visit your class.

Activity #3
    Transition: "The book we are about to read is about a dog-wolf named White Fang. It tells about how he is born and lives in the wild and through contact with humans makes the transition from life in the wild to a domesticated life with man."

    Distribute the materials students will use in this unit. Explain in detail how students are to use these materials.

    Study Guides Students should read the study guide questions for each reading assignment prior to beginning the reading assignment to get a feeling for what events and ideas are important in the section they are about to read. After reading the section, students will (as a class or individually) answer the questions to review the important events and ideas from that section of the book. Students should keep the study guides as study materials for the unit test.

<u>Vocabulary</u>   Prior to reading a reading assignment, students will do vocabulary work related to the section of the book they are about to read. Following the completion of the reading of the book, there will be a vocabulary review of all the words used in the vocabulary assignments. Students should keep their vocabulary work as study materials for the unit test.

<u>Reading Assignment Sheet</u>   You need to fill in the reading assignment sheet to let students know by when their reading has to be completed. You can either write the assignment sheet up on a side blackboard or bulletin board and leave it there for students to see each day, or you can "ditto" copies for each student to have. In either case, you should advise students to become very familiar with the reading assignments so they know what is expected of them.

<u>Extra Activities Center</u>   The Unit Resource portion of this unit contains suggestions for an extra library of related books and articles in your classroom as well as crossword and word search puzzles. Make an extra activities center in your room where you will keep these materials for students to use. (Bring the books and articles in from the library and keep several copies of the puzzles on hand.) Explain to students that these materials are available for students to use when they finish reading assignments or other class work early.

<u>Nonfiction Assignment Sheet</u>   Explain to students that they each are to read at least one non-fiction piece from the in-class library at some time during the unit. Students will fill out a nonfiction assignment sheet after completing the reading to help you (the teacher) evaluate their reading experiences and to help the students think about and evaluate their own reading experiences.

<u>Books</u>   Each school has its own rules and regulations regarding student use of school books. Advise students of the procedures that are normal for your school.

<u>Activity #4</u>
Tell students to preview the study questions and have students do the vocabulary work for Chapters I-III of *White Fang*. If students do not finish this assignment during this class period, they should complete it prior to the next class meeting.

NONFICTION ASSIGNMENT SHEET
(To be completed after reading the required nonfiction article)

Name _____ Date _____

Title of Nonfiction Read _____

Written By _____ Publication Date _____

I. Factual Summary: Write a short summary of the piece you read.

II. Vocabulary
    1. With which vocabulary words in the piece did you encounter some degree of difficulty?

    2. How did you resolve your lack of understanding with these words?

III. Interpretation: What was the main point the author wanted you to get from reading his work?

IV. Criticism
    1. With which points of the piece did you agree or find easy to accept? Why?

    2. With which points of the piece did you disagree or find difficult to believe? Why?

V. Personal Response: What do you think about this piece? OR How does this piece influence your ideas?

LESSON TWO

Objectives
1. To read chapters I-III
2. To give students practice reading orally
3. To evaluate students' oral reading

Activity

Have students read chapters I-III of *White Fang* out loud in class. You probably know the best way to get readers with your class; pick students at random, ask for volunteers, or use whatever method works best for your group. If you have not yet completed an oral reading evaluation for your students this marking period, this would be a good opportunity to do so. A form is included with this unit for your convenience.

If students do not complete reading chapters 1-3 in class, they should do so prior to your next class meeting.

LESSON THREE

Objectives
1. To preview the study questions and vocabulary for chapters IV-VII
2. To read chapters IV-VII orally
3. To complete the oral reading evaluations

Activity #1

Give students about fifteen minutes to preview the study questions for chapters IV-VII of *White Fang* and to do the related vocabulary work.

Activity #2

Have students read chapters IV-VII of *White Fang* orally in class. Continue (and try to complete) the oral reading evaluations.

ORAL READING EVALUATION - *White Fang*

Name _____ Class____ Date _____

SKILL	EXCELLENT	GOOD	AVERAGE	FAIR	POOR
Fluency	5	4	3	2	1
Clarity	5	4	3	2	1
Audibility	5	4	3	2	1
Pronunciation	5	4	3	2	1
_____	5	4	3	2	1
_____	5	4	3	2	1

Total _____   Grade _____

Comments:

LESSON FOUR

Objectives
1. To review the main ideas and events from chapters I-VII
2. To preview the study questions and vocabulary for chapters VIII-XI
3. To read chapters VIII-XI

Activity #1

Give students a few minutes to formulate answers for the study guide questions for chapters I-VII, and then discuss the answers to the questions in detail. Write the answers on the board or overhead transparency so students can have the correct answers for study purposes. Note: It is a good practice in public speaking and leadership skills for individual students to take charge of leading the discussions of the study questions. Perhaps a different student could go to the front of the class and lead the discussion each day that the study questions are discussed during this unit. Of course, the teacher should guide the discussion when appropriate and be sure to fill in any gaps the students leave.

Activity #2

Give students about fifteen minutes to preview the study questions for chapters VIII-XI of *White Fang* and to do the related vocabulary work.

Activity #3

Have students read chapters VIII-XI of *White Fang* silently in class. If students do not complete this assignment during class, they should do so prior to the next class period.

LESSON FIVE

<u>Objectives</u>
1. To review the main ideas and events from chapters VIII-XI
2. To give students the opportunity to express their personal opinions in writing
3. To give the teacher the opportunity to evaluate students' writing skills
4. To introduce the theme of civilization/domestication

<u>Activity #1</u>
Give students a few minutes to formulate answers for the study guide questions for chapters VIII-XI, and then discuss the answers to the questions in detail. Write the answers on the board or overhead transparency so students can have the correct answers for study purposes.

<u>Activity #2</u>
Distribute Writing Assignment #1. Discuss the directions in detail and give students ample time to complete the assignment.

<u>Activity #3</u>
Tell students that prior to your next class period they should have completed the prereading work and the reading of chapters XII-XV. If students finish the writing assignment early, they may begin this reading assignment.

WRITING ASSIGNMENT #1 - *White Fang*

PROMPT

The animals we most often come in contact with have been domesticated; they are no longer wild. And "civilization" is sweeping away the natural habitat of the remaining wild animals on our planet. Yet, if you look closely at our "civilization," we see people killing, maiming, mugging, raping and fighting each other at an alarming rate. Are we truly civilized?

Your assignment is to answer this question, "What does it mean to be civilized?"

PREWRITNG

This assignment is designed so you can answer with your own opinion; there is no perfectly "right" or "wrong" answer. One way to approach this assignment is to think about what characteristics you expect from a group of people who are "civilized." Jot down those characteristics. This is one way to create a definition: definition by example.

DRAFTING

Start with a paragraph in which you introduce the idea of civilization. The paragraphs in the body of your paper could/should each introduce and explain the characteristics you have jotted down, one characteristic explained in each paragraph. Finish your paper with a paragraph that sums up the many parts you have set forth.

PROMPT

When you finish the rough draft of your paper, ask a student who sits near you to read it. After reading your rough draft, he/she should tell you what he/she liked best about your work, which parts were difficult to understand, and ways in which your work could be improved. Reread your paper considering your critic's comments, and make the corrections you think are necessary.

PROOFREADING

Do a final proofreading of your paper double-checking your grammar, spelling, organization, and the clarity of your ideas.

LESSON SIX

Objectives
1. To review the main events and ideas from chapters XII-XV
2. To preview the study questions for chapters XVI-XIX
3. To familiarize students with the vocabulary in chapters XVI-XIX
4. To read chapters XVI-XIX

Activity #1

Use the study questions for chapters XII-XV as a quiz to evaluate whether students did the required reading and, if they did, how well they understood what they read. After students have a few minutes to answer the questions, discuss the answers to the questions as a class.

Activity #2

Give students about fifteen minutes to preview the study questions for chapters XVI-XIX of *White Fang* and to do the related vocabulary work.

Activity #3

Students should then read chapters XVI-XIX silently in class. If they do not complete this assignment during this class period, they should do so prior to your next class period.

LESSON SEVEN

Objectives
1. To review the main events and ideas from chapters XVI-XIX
2. To preview the study questions for chapters XX-XXII
3. To familiarize students with the vocabulary in chapters XX-XXII
4. To read chapters XX-XXII

Activity #1

Give students a few minutes to formulate answers to the study questions for chapters XVI-XIX. After students have a few minutes to answer the questions, discuss the answers to the questions as a class.

Activity #2

Give students about fifteen minutes to preview the study questions for chapters XX-XXII of *White Fang* and to do the related vocabulary work.

Activity #3

Students should then read chapters XX-XXII silently in class. If they do not complete this assignment during this class period, they should do so prior to your next class period.

LESSON EIGHT

Objectives
1. To review the main events and ideas from chapters XX-XXII
2. To preview the study questions for chapters XXIII-XXV
3. To familiarize students with the vocabulary in chapters XXIII-XXV
4. To read chapters XXIII-XXV

Activity #1
Give students a few minutes to formulate answers to the study questions for chapters XX-XXII. After students have a few minutes to answer the questions, discuss the answers to the questions as a class.

Activity #2
Give students about fifteen minutes to preview the study questions for chapters XXIII-XXV of *White Fang* and to do the related vocabulary work.

Activity #3
Students should then read chapters XXIII-XXV silently in class. If they do not complete this assignment during this class period, they should do so prior to your next class period.

LESSON NINE

Objectives
1. To review the main ideas and events from chapters XXIII-XXV
2. To discuss *White Fang* on interpretive and critical levels

Activity #1
Take a few minutes at the beginning of the period to review the study questions for chapters XXIII-XXV.

Activity #2
Choose the questions from the Extra Discussion Questions/Writing Assignments which seem most appropriate for your students. A class discussion of these questions is most effective if students have been given the opportunity to formulate answers to the questions prior to the discussion. To this end, you may either have all the students formulate answers to all the questions, divide your class into groups and assign one or more questions to each group, or you could assign one question to each student in your class. The option you choose will make a difference in the amount of class time needed for this activity.

Activity #3
After students have had ample time to formulate answers to the questions, begin your class discussion of the questions and the ideas presented by the questions. Be sure students take notes during the discussion so they have information to study for the unit test.

EXTRA WRITING ASSIGNMENTS/DISCUSSION QUESTIONS - *White Fang*

Interpretation

1. Explain the significance of the title of *White Fang* considering that he doesn't even appear in the first third of the book.

2. Is the story of *White Fang* believable? Explain why or why not.

3. Explain how White Fang changes during the course of the novel.

4. Where is the climax of the story? Explain your choice.

5. Describe the law of the survival of the fittest. Give examples from the story depicting this law in action.

6. List in order the times White Fang injures or kills someone or something in the book and explain what he learns (if anything) from each incident.

7. What are the conflicts in the story and how are they resolved?

8. What does "adapt" mean? Give all the examples of it that you can find in this book.

9. From what point of view is the story written? How does that affect our attitudes as we read?

Critical

10. Compare and contrast Gray Beaver, Beauty Smith and Weedon Scott.

11. List ways in which White Fang was able to adapt to being civilized.

12. What was Judge Scott's role in the story?

13. What of White Fang's "wild" instincts helped him to survive as he became civilized?

14. Why was White Fang's relationship with Weedon Scott important? List examples showing the progression of their relationship.

15. Discuss the idea of the "man-god" as it relates to the novel.

16. What is anthropomorphism? Explain its use in *White Fang*.

White Fang Extra Discussion Questions Page 2

Critical Continued

17. Why did Jack London include the part of the story about the she-wolf and One Eye?

18. What messages are presented to the reader of this book?

19. Explain the significance of each chapter's title.

20. How does civilization compare to life in the wild in this story?

21. What effect did Liplip and the puppy pack have on White Fang?

22. This book is full of actions which evoke responses. Give at least five examples.

23. How was White Fang's fight with Cherokee important to the novel?

24. Why were the incidents showing White Fang's bravery and loyalty at the end of the story important?

25. What are the characteristics of "naturalistic" writing, and how does *White Fang* demonstrate those characteristics?

Personal Response

26. What "wild" instincts are present in people, and what purposes do they serve?

27. White Fang's life changed considerably during the course of the novel. Sometimes things happen in our lives and we just have to deal with the change, pick up and move on with life. What are some of those kinds of events that affect our lives?

28. Did you enjoy reading the story *White Fang*? Why or why not?

29. Suppose White Fang had not recovered from his wounds at the end of the story. How would that have changed the message of the book?

LESSON TEN

Objective
 To review all of the vocabulary work done in this unit

Activity
 Choose one (or more) of the vocabulary review activities listed below and spend your class period as directed in the activity. Some of the materials for these review activities are located in the Vocabulary Resource section in this unit.

VOCABULARY REVIEW ACTIVITIES

1. Divide your class into two teams and have an old-fashioned spelling or definition bee.

2. Give each of your students (or students in groups of two, three or four) a *White Fang* Vocabulary Word Search Puzzle. The person (group) to find all of the vocabulary words in the puzzle first wins.

3. Give students a *White Fang* Vocabulary Word Search Puzzle without the word list. The person or group to find the most vocabulary words in the puzzle wins.

4. Use a *White Fang* Vocabulary Crossword Puzzle. Put the puzzle onto a transparency on the overhead projector (so everyone can see it), and do the puzzle together as a class.

5. Give students a *White Fang* Vocabulary Matching Worksheet to do.

6. Divide your class into two teams. Use the *White Fang* vocabulary words with their letters jumbled as a word list. Student 1 from Team A faces off against Student 1 from Team B. You write the first jumbled word on the board. The first student (1A or 1B) to unscramble the word wins the chance for his/her team to score points. If 1A wins the jumble, go to student 2A and give him/her a definition. He/she must give you the correct spelling of the vocabulary word which fits that definition. If he/she does, Team A scores a point, and you give student 3A a definition for which you expect a correctly spelled matching vocabulary word. Continue giving Team A definitions until some team member makes an incorrect response. An incorrect response sends the game back to the jumbled-word face off, this time with students 2A and 2B. Instead of repeating giving definitions to the first few students of each team, continue with the student after the one who gave the last incorrect response on the team. For example, if Team B wins the jumbled-word face-off, and student 5B gave the last incorrect answer for Team B, you would start this round of definition questions with student 6B, and so on. The team with the most points wins!

7. Have students write a story in which they correctly use as many vocabulary words as possible. Have students read their compositions orally! Post the most original compositions on your bulletin board!

LESSON ELEVEN

Objectives
    1. To give students a brief introduction to the world of advertising and persuasion
    2. To prepare students for the project they will be assigned to do
    3. To introduce students to their project assignments

NOTE: Prior to this lesson you need to purchase, rent or create a video tape with five or six different commercials on it. Also, purchase, rent or create an audio cassette with five or six radio commercials on it.

Activity #1
    Show the video tape of commercials.

Activity #2
    Transition: "What you have just seen is probably nothing new to you. We are bombarded with advertisements/commercials every time we turn on the television set. Television commercials are just one facet of the advertising business. There are magazine ads, billboards, radio commercials, direct mail ads, and newspaper ads; there are even advertisements on grocery carts at some supermarkets. Advertising is everywhere.
    What is advertising? (Get some student responses.) Advertising is persuasion. Someone wants you to buy their product or believe in a cause or behave in a certain way."
    Get students to give you examples of: advertisements to persuade you to buy a product, advertisements to get you to believe in a cause, and advertisements to make you want to behave in a certain way.

Activity #3
    "Advertising is a huge industry. Businesses and agencies hire advertising agents -- marketing specialists to make their products sell or to get their messages across. So how do they do it? Those marketing specialists don't just wave a magic wand and POOF! the whole country wants to drink Pepsi Cola. No, it is planned--engineered very carefully for the desired effect."
    Take time now to look again at the commercial video. Ask students what elements they find in the ads. To whom does the ad appeal? How? Why? Develop a list of characteristics that are common to all the ads.
    After you complete looking at the video of commercials, turn your attention to magazine, newspaper and radio ads. Have students investigate how they are put together and write down their characteristics.

Activity #4
    Distribute the Project Assignment Sheets. Discuss the directions in detail. Telll students to think about the project overnight and to try do decide on a topic before the next class period.

PROJECT ASSIGNMENT SHEET - *White Fang*

PROMPT
The project is to create an advertisement.

This project will be done in several parts. You have already taken the first step by learning some basic information about how advertisements work. Next you will need to choose a topic. Following that, you need to decide whether you want to work independently on in a group. Other steps will be to go to the library and do some research about your topic, decide on the media for your advertisement, plan out the best way to do your ad, actually produce the ad, and introduce your ad to an audience.

CHOOSING A TOPIC
The topic you choose must in some way relate to *White Fang*. Here are some suggestions for topics, but feel free to think of one of your own:
    a. Protect the environment
    b. Protect wild animals
    c. Recycle
    d. Care properly for pets
    e. Be more civilized: 1. Don't do drugs
                                 2. Stop violence in our homes
                                 3. Stop violence in our streets
                                 4. Stop killing each other
    f. Donate to a wildlife fund (pick a specific one)
    g. Buy our product to prevent burglaries (Think of a specific product.)
    h. Use our product when you get back to nature and go camping in the wild (Think
       of a specific product.)

CHOOSING THE MEDIA
Since you will actually be producing the advertisement, consider carefully what form you want your advertisement to take. You could make a television commercial (videotaped), a radio advertisement (recorded on a cassette tape), a magazine, newspaper or direct mail advertisement (completed on paper).

CHOOSING PARTNERS
You may do your project independently, or you may team up with other students in the class who have an interest in exploring the same topic you wish to explore. If you do a group project, all individuals in the group must contribute to the research, planning and production.

LESSON TWELVE

Objectives
    1. To get students started on their projects
    2. To give students the opportunity to do the necessary research for their projects

Activity #1
    Tell students to write down their names and the topic for their projects on slips of paper. Collect the papers. Find students who have the same interests and ask them if they wish to work individually or as a group. Make a list of those students who decide to work together.

Activity #2
    Take students to the library. Explain that students are to find whatever information they can about their topics. If students plan to market widgets, for example, they should find out everything they can about the widgets and the market for whom the widgets are intended. If students want people to donate to a charity, they should find out all they can about that charity. And so on.
    Explain to students that this research also fulfills their Nonfiction Reading Assignment. Students should take good notes about their research because they will be expected to use that information in the next writing assignment.
    Also, students should fill out their Nonfiction Reading Assignment Sheets.

LESSON THIRTEEN

Objectives
    1. To give students the opportunity to practice writing to inform
    2. To check students research
    3. To make sure that all group members are contributing
    4. To give the teacher the opportunity to evaluate students' writing skills

Activity
    Distribute Writing Assignment #3. Discuss the directions in detail and give students ample time to complete the assignment. If students finish the writing assignment early, they should continue working on their projects.

WRITING ASSIGNMENT #3 - *White Fang*

PROMPT
You have done your research for the project assignment. Now you are to write a composition in which you summarize your research. This is to help you review and analyze the information as well as to evaluate the success of your research.

PREWRITING
Your research has been done, and you probably have a stack of notes on paper sitting in front of you. Look at your notes and begin to organize them. You will probably be able to see that your notes fall into several categories of information. Jot down what those categories are. Arrange your notes so that the information from each category appears together. Now arrange the categories in an order that makes sense.

DRAFTING
Start with a paragraph in which you introduce your topic. Write one paragraph for each of the categories of information you have, including the information in your notes within the paragraphs. Write a paragraph in which you state the conclusions your data suggests.

PROMPT
When you finish the rough draft of your paper, ask a student who sits near you to read it. After reading your rough draft, he/she should tell you what he/she liked best about your work, which parts were difficult to understand, and ways in which your work could be improved. Reread your paper considering your critic's comments, and make the corrections you think are necessary.

PROOFREADING
Do a final proofreading of your paper double-checking your grammar, spelling, organization, and the clarity of your ideas.

LESSON FOURTEEN

Objective
    To give students time to plan their advertisements

Activity
    Give students this class period to plan their advertisements.

NOTE: This would be a good time to also have private writing conferences with individual students.

LESSONS FIFTEEN AND SIXTEEN

Objective
    To give students time to produce their advertisements

Activity
    Make the necessary equipment (video cameras, cassette tape recorders, etc.) available to students for the production of their advertisements.

LESSON SEVENTEEN

Objectives
    1. To bring the projects to a conclusion
    2. To give students the opportunity to proudly show off their advertisements
    3. To broaden students' knowledge about our world

Activity
    Take this class period to view all of the advertisements your students have produced.

LESSON EIGHTEEN

Objective
    To review all the material from this unit

Activity
    Choose one of the review activities included with this unit and spend your class period as directed in that activity.

WRITING EVALUATION FORM - *White Fang*

Name _____ Date _____

Grade _____

Circle One For Each Item:

Grammar: excellent   good   fair   poor

Spelling: excellent   good   fair   poor

Punctuation: excellent   good   fair   poor

Legibility: excellent   good   fair   poor

Strengths:

Weaknesses:

Comments/Suggestions:

PROJECT EVALUATION SHEET - *White Fang*

Name(s) _____

Topic of Advertisement _____

Score _____   Grade _____

Persuasiveness	1	2	3	4	5
Creativity	1	2	3	4	5
Production Mechanics	1	2	3	4	5
_____	1	2	3	4	5
_____	1	2	3	4	5
_____	1	2	3	4	5

Total _____

Comments:

REVIEW GAMES/ACTIVITIES - *White Fang*

1. Ask the class to make up a unit test for *White Fang*. The test should have 4 sections: matching, true/false, short answer, and essay. Students may use 1/2 period to make the test and then swap papers and use the other 1/2 class period to take a test a classmate has devised. (open book) You may want to use the unit test included in this guide or take questions from the students' unit tests to formulate your own test.

2. Take 1/2 period for students to make up true and false questions (including the answers). Collect the papers and divide the class into two teams. Draw a big tic-tac-toe board on the chalk board. Make one team X and one team O. Ask questions to each side, giving each student one turn. If the question is answered correctly, that students' team's letter (X or O) is placed in the box. If the answer is incorrect, no mark is placed in the box. The object is to get three marks in a row like tic-tac-toe. You may want to keep track of the number of games won for each team.

3. Take 1/2 period for students to make up questions (true/false and short answer). Collect the questions. Divide the class into two teams. You'll alternate asking questions to individual members of teams A & B (like in a spelling bee). The question keeps going from A to B until it is correctly answered, then a new question is asked. A correct answer does not allow the team to get another question. Correct answers are +2 points; incorrect answers are -1 point.

4. Have students pair up and quiz each other from their study guides and class notes.

5. Give students a *White Fang* crossword puzzle to complete.

6. Divide your class into two teams. Use the *White Fang* crossword words with their letters jumbled as a word list. Student 1 from Team A faces off against Student 1 from Team B. You write the first jumbled word on the board. The first student (1A or 1B) to unscramble the word wins the chance for his/her team to score points. If 1A wins the jumble, go to student 2A and give him/her a clue. He/she must give you the correct word which matches that clue. If he/she does, Team A scores a point, and you give student 3A a clue for which you expect another correct response. Continue giving Team A clues until some team member makes an incorrect response. An incorrect response sends the game back to the jumbled-word face off, this time with students 2A and 2B. Instead of repeating giving clues to the first few students of each team, continue with the student after the one who gave the last incorrect response on the team. For example, if Team B wins the jumbled-word face-off, and student 5B gave the last incorrect answer for Team B, you would start this round of clue questions with student 6B, and so on. The team with the most points wins!

UNIT TESTS

SHORT ANSWER UNIT TEST #1 - *White Fang*

I. Matching

___ Gray Beaver   A. White Fang's father

___ Cherokee   B. Saved White Fang

___ Beauty Smith   C. White Fang's Indian master

___ One Eye   D. The gray cub

___ Mit-sah   E. Is saved by White Fang

___ Jim Hall   F. Tormented & used White Fang to make money

___ Weedon Scott   G. Weedon Scott's friend/helper

___ White Fang   H. White Fang's mother; she-wolf

___ Judge Scott   I. Gray Beaver's son

___ Kiche   J. Dog in Gray Beaver's camp

___ Lip-lip   K. Bulldog who fought White Fang

___ Matt   L. Tried to kill the judge

II. Short Answer

1. Identify Bill and Henry.

2. How was Henry saved?

3. What happened to One Eye?

White Fang Short Answer Unit Test 1 Page 2

4. How did White Fang differentiate man from beast?

5. What fighting technique did White Fang successfully use?

6. Why did White Fang become afraid in the wild?

7. Why did White Fang defend Mit-sah?

8. What was the difference between White Fang and the other dogs?

9. How did White Fang escape punishment for killing the white men's dogs?

10. Why did Gray Beaver sell White Fang?

White Fang Short Answer Unit Test 1 Page 3

11. Why did White Fang kill Major?

12. Why didn't Matt kill White Fang?

13. Who tried to steal White Fang? Why wasn't he successful?

14. How did White Fang feel about the city?

15. Why did White Fang kill the dogs at the crossroads?

White Fang Short Answer Unit Test 1 Page 4

III. Essay

    White Fang had several owners throughout his life. Explain how each owner's characteristics correlate to a stage from White Fang's savage (wild) life to his civilized (domesticated) life.

IV. Vocabulary

    Write down the words given orally and then go back and write down their definitions.

1.

2.

3.

4.

5.

6.

7.

8.

9.

10.

KEY: SHORT ANSWER UNIT TEST #1 - *White Fang*

I. Matching

  _C_ Gray Beaver   A. White Fang's father

  _K_ Cherokee   B. Saved White Fang

  _F_ Beauty Smith   C. White Fang's Indian master

  _A_ One Eye   D. The gray cub

  _I_ Mit-sah   E. Is saved by White Fang

  _L_ Jim Hall   F. Tormented & used White Fang to make money

  _B_ Weedon Scott   G. Weedon Scott's friend/helper

  _D_ White Fang   H. White Fang's mother; she-wolf

  _E_ Judge Scott   I. Gray Beaver's son

  _H_ Kiche   J. Dog in Gray Beaver's camp

  _J_ Lip-lip   K. Bulldog who fought White Fang

  _G_ Matt   L. Tried to kill the judge

II. Short Answer

1. Identify Bill and Henry.
    They were the men at the beginning of the story who lost their dogs to the she-wolf and her pack.

2. How was Henry saved?
    Some men with sleds were traveling by and happened to see him. They gave him transportation.

3. What happened to One Eye?
    He was killed by the lynx.

4. How did White Fang differentiate man from beast?
    Man didn't fight with fangs and claws; rather, he used "dead" things like clubs and guns.

5. What fighting technique did White Fang successfully use?
    He learned to use the element of surprise.

6. Why did White Fang become afraid in the wild?
    He had spent so much time in the care of men that he had forgotten what to do in the wild; life with men was much easier.

7. Why did White Fang defend Mit-sah?
    Although the fight between the boys and Mit-sah was no concern of his, White Fang defended Mit-sah out of duty to his master.

8. What was the difference between White Fang and the other dogs?
    The other dogs had been domesticated for several generations; White Fang had come directly from the wild.

9. How did White Fang escape punishment for killing the white men's dogs?
    He would pick a fight with a dog, overthrow it, and let the rest of the pack come in to finish it off. White Fang would then run away, leaving the pack to take the punishment for killing the dog.

10. Why did Gray Beaver sell White Fang?
    He had become an alcoholic and sold White Fang for some bottles of whiskey.

11. Why did White Fang kill Major?
    He killed Major because Major tried to take his meat.

12. Why didn't Matt kill White Fang?
    Every time he put the rifle to his shoulder, White Fang would growl and bristle. When he put the rifle down, White Fang would respond by becoming calmer. Matt and Weedon Scott realized that White Fang was too smart to kill.

13. Who tried to steal White Fang? Why wasn't he successful?
    Beauty Smith tried to steal White Fang, but White Fang attacked him (and probably would have killed him had Weedon Scott not intervened).

14. How did White Fang feel about the city?
    He hated it. It was too confusing and frightening, and it made him feel small.

15. Why did White Fang kill the dogs at the crossroads?

> The dogs at the crossroads always taunted White Fang who would never fight back because his master had told him not to fight. One day the owners of the dogs sicced them onto White Fang, whose owner gave him permission to fight. So, White Fang fought them and killed them.

III. Essay — White Fang had several owners throughout his life. Explain how each owner's characteristics correlate to a stage from White Fang's savage (wild) life to his civilized (domesticated) life.

IV. Vocabulary - Choose ten of the vocabulary words to read orally for your students to write down.

SHORT ANSWER UNIT TEST 2 - *White Fang*

I. Matching

___ Gray Beaver   A. Weedon Scott's friend/helper

___ Cherokee   B. Is saved by White Fang

___ Beauty Smith   C. Saved White Fang

___ One Eye   D. The gray cub

___ Mit-sah   E. White Fang's Indian master

___ Jim Hall   F. Gray Beaver's son

___ Weedon Scott   G. White Fang's father

___ White Fang   H. Dog in Gray Beaver's camp

___ Judge Scott   I. Tormented & used White Fang to make money

___ Kiche   J. White Fang's mother; she-wolf

___ Lip-lip   K. Tried to kill the judge

___ Matt   L. Bulldog who fought White Fang

II. Short Answer

1. Why was the gray pup confused about the white wall?

2. How did White Fang differentiate man from beast?

3. What was the "crime of crimes"?

White Fang Short Answer Unit Test 2 Page 2

4. What fighting technique did White Fang successfully use?

5. Why did White Fang become afraid in the wild?

6. Why was White Fang afraid of hands?

7. How did White Fang escape punishment for killing the white men's dogs?

8. For what did Beauty Smith use White Fang?

9. Why didn't Matt kill White Fang?

White Fang Short Answer Unit Test 2 Page 3

10. What was so important about White Fang's snuggling?

11. Where was Weedon Scott going, and why did he decide to take White Fang?

12. Why did White Fang kill the dogs at the crossroads?

III. Composition
   Explain the stages White Fang went through as he changed from a wild animal to a domestic pet.

White Fang Short Answer Unit Test 2 Page 4

IV. Vocabulary

    Listen to the vocabulary words and write them down. Go back later and write down the correct definitions next to the words.

1.

2.

3.

4.

5.

6.

7.

8.

9.

10.

KEY: SHORT ANSWER UNIT TEST 2 - *White Fang*

I. Matching

__E__ Gray Beaver   A. Weedon Scott's friend/helper

__L__ Cherokee   B. Is saved by White Fang

__I__ Beauty Smith   C. Saved White Fang

__G__ One Eye   D. The gray cub

__F__ Mit-sah   E. White Fang's Indian master

__K__ Jim Hall   F. Gray Beaver's son

__C__ Weedon Scott   G. White Fang's father

__D__ White Fang   H. Dog in Gray Beaver's camp

__B__ Judge Scott   I. Tormented & used White Fang to make money

__J__ Kiche   J. White Fang's mother; she-wolf

__H__ Lip-lip   K. Tried to kill the judge

__A__ Matt   L. Bulldog who fought White Fang

II. Short Answer

1. Why was the gray pup confused about the white wall?
    He saw that his father could disappear into the white wall. Since he was not allowed to go near the white wall, he tried his father's trick on the other walls but only managed to get a sore nose. The white wall remained a mystery to him.

2. How did White Fang differentiate man from beast?
    Man didn't fight with fangs and claws; rather, he used "dead" things like clubs and guns.

3. What was the "crime of crimes"?
    Biting a man was absolutely forbidden.

4. What fighting technique did White Fang successfully use?
   He learned to use the element of surprise.

5. Why did White Fang become afraid in the wild?
   He had spent so much time in the care of men that he had forgotten what to do in the wild; life with men was much easier.

6. Why was White Fang afraid of hands?
   Hands controlled whips and clubs to hurt dogs.

7. How did White Fang escape punishment for killing the white men's dogs?
   He would pick a fight with a dog, overthrow it, and let the rest of the pack come in to finish it off. White Fang would then run away, leaving the pack to take the punishment for killing the dog.

8. For what did Beauty Smith use White Fang?
   He used him as a fighting dog. He tormented White Fang to keep him in a constant rage so people who would come to see him fight would get their money's worth.

9. Why didn't Matt kill White Fang?
   Every time he put the rifle to his shoulder, White Fang would growl and bristle. When he put the rifle down, White Fang would respond by becoming calmer. Matt and Weedon Scott realized that White Fang was too smart to kill.

10. What was so important about White Fang's snuggling?
    He was saying, "You have my total confidence." This, from a dog who had formerly been vicious.

11. Where was Weedon Scott going, and why did he decide to take White Fang?
    He was going to California. He decided to take White Fang with him because he knew that White Fang would starve himself to death if he could not go with his master. The final decision came when White Fang jumped through glass to be with his master.

12. Why did White Fang kill the dogs at the crossroads?
    The dogs at the crossroads always taunted White Fang who would never fight back because his master had told him not to fight. One day the owners of the dogs sicced them onto White Fang, whose owner gave him permission to fight. So, White Fang fought them and killed them.

III. Composition Answers will vary

IV. Vocabulary Choose ten vocabulary words to dictate to your students for this part of the test.

ADVANCED SHORT ANSWER UNIT TEST - *White Fang*

I. Matching

___ Gray Beaver   A. Weedon Scott's friend/helper

___ Cherokee   B. Is saved by White Fang

___ Beauty Smith   C. Saved White Fang

___ One Eye   D. The gray cub

___ Mit-sah   E. White Fang's Indian master

___ Jim Hall   F. Gray Beaver's son

___ Weedon Scott   G. White Fang's father

___ White Fang   H. Dog in Gray Beaver's camp

___ Judge Scott   I. Tormented & used White Fang to make money

___ Kiche   J. White Fang's mother; she-wolf

___ Lip-lip   K. Tried to kill the judge

___ Matt   L. Bulldog who fought White Fang

II. Composition
1. Compare and contrast Gray Beaver, Beauty Smith and Weedon Scott.

White Fang Advanced Short Answer Unit Test Page 2

2. Discuss the idea of the man-god as it relates to the novel.

3. Explain the stages through which White Fang passed as he became domesticated.

4. Why was the part of the book about the she-wolf and One Eye included?

White Fang Advanced Short Answer Unit Test Page 3

5. Where is the climax of the story? Explain your choice.

6. What is the law of the survival of the fittest? Give 4 examples of it from the text of *White Fang*.

White Fang Advanced Short Answer Unit Test Page 4

III. Vocabulary

    Listen to the vocabulary words and write them down. Go back later and write a composition in which you use all of the vocabulary words. The composition must relate in some way to *White Fang*.

MULTIPLE CHOICE UNIT TEST 1 - *White Fang*

I. Matching

___ Gray Beaver   A. White Fang's father

___ Cherokee   B. Saved White Fang

___ Beauty Smith   C. White Fang's Indian master

___ One Eye   D. The gray cub

___ Mit-sah   E. Is saved by White Fang

___ Jim Hall   F. Tormented & used White Fang to make money

___ Weedon Scott   G. Weedon Scott's friend/helper

___ White Fang   H. White Fang's mother; she-wolf

___ Judge Scott   I. Gray Beaver's son

___ Kiche   J. Dog in Gray Beaver's camp

___ Lip-lip   K. Bulldog who fought White Fang

___ Matt   L. Tried to kill the judge

White Fang Multiple Choice Test 1 Page 2

II. Multiple Choice

1. Where does this story take place?
   a. In the far North
   b. In Greenland
   c. In Iceland
   d. In Russia

2. What happened when Bill tried to save One Ear?
   a. Bill barely managed to save One Ear.
   b. One Ear turned on him.
   c. Both Bill and One Ear were eaten.
   d. One Ear saved them both.

3. What confused the gray pup?
   a. The white wall
   b. The floor
   c. The snow
   d. The lynx

4. What happened to One Eye?
   a. The she-wolf got mad and killed him.
   b. The lynx killed him.
   c. He went away as was the custom of the male wolves.
   d. Hunters killed him.

5. How did White Fang differentiate man from beast?
   a. Man walked on his hind legs.
   b. Man had fire.
   c. Man smelled different.
   d. Man fought with clubs and guns.

6. What was the "crime of crimes"?
   a. Leaving man
   b. Biting man
   c. Disobeying man
   d. Stealing from man

7. What fighting technique did White Fang successfully use?
   a. Surprise
   b. Feigning
   c. Holding the throat
   d. Clawing

White Fang Multiple Choice Test 1 Page 3

8. Why did White Fang return to Gray Beaver?
    a. Gray Beaver came after him and forced him to return.
    b. Life with man was much easier than life in the wild.
    c. He couldn't find his mother.
    d. He was wounded.

9. Why was White Fang afraid of hands?
    a. They looked strange.
    b. They were always moving.
    c. They often held clubs and whips.
    d. He didn't understand them.

10. What did White Fang think of the "white gods"?
    a. He liked them.
    b. The thought they were not very smart.
    c. He trusted them.
    d. They were more powerful than the Indians.

11. Why did Gray Beaver sell White Fang?
    a. He wanted whiskey.
    b. He was tired of retrieving White Fang from the wild.
    c. He decided to move away and couldn't take White Fang with him.
    d. White Fang was nothing but trouble for him.

12. Why did White Fang always win his fights?
    a. He fought only smaller, domesticated dogs.
    b. Beauty wouldn't take a fight he didn't know White Fang could win.
    c. The experiences of his life had made him a skillful fighter.
    d. The fights were "fixed."

13. Why didn't Matt kill White Fang?
    a. He missed; White Fang got away.
    b. He was out of ammunition.
    c. He realized White Fang was too smart to kill.
    d. He didn't have the nerve.

14. What did White Fang do when Weedon Scott left in the spring?
    a. He went to look for his master.
    b. He would not eat and became sick.
    c. He carried on "as usual."
    d. He ran away back to the wild.

White Fang Multiple Choice Test 1 Page 4

15. What was so important about White Fang's snuggling?
    a. It kept Weedon Smith warm.
    b. It helped him get well.
    c. It showed his total confidence in Weedon Scott.
    d. It was his way of saying he was lonely.

16. Why wouldn't White Fang fight the Collie?
    a. His fighting days were over.
    b. He didn't want to kill the Judge's dog.
    c. He was afraid of her.
    d. His instincts would not let him fight a female.

17. Why did White Fang kill the dogs at the crossroads?
    a. They took his food.
    b. They attacked the Judge.
    c. The dogs attacked the collie.
    d. The dogs had taunted White Fang, and given permission to fight.

18. Why did White Fang leave the injured Weedon Scott in the woods?
    a. He went to chase a rabbit.
    b. His master told him to go.
    c. He didn't realize his master was injured.
    d. He got confused.

19. What happened to White Fang?
    a. He lived happily ever after with the Scotts and the collie.
    b. He died from wounds he got while saving the judge.
    c. He eventually returned to the wild.
    d. He was put to sleep.

White Fang Multiple Choice Test 1 Page 5

III. Vocabulary

___ 1. Myriad
___ 2. Prodigious
___ 3. Interminably
___ 4. Tenacity
___ 5. Guise
___ 6. Ponderous
___ 7. Auspiciously
___ 8. Gregarious
___ 9. Adverse
___ 10. Intrepidity
___ 11. Indomitable
___ 12. Appurtenances
___ 13. Burgeoning
___ 14. Ostentatious
___ 15. Abashed
___ 16. Enmity
___ 17. Profusely
___ 18. Impregnable
___ 19. Culminating
___ 20. Abasement

A. a countless number, innumerable
B. toughness
C. irrepressible; invincible
D. hostility, opposition
E. favorably
F. endlessly
G. massive and awkward
H. vain, pomp, ambitious display
I. fearless, bold
J. blossoming, growing
K. behavior
L. opposed to; against
M. lavishly, exuberantly
M. reaching the highest point
O. huge, enormous
P. ashamed
Q. appendages
R. living in a pack, not solitary
S. able to resist attack, invincible
T. disgraced

MULTIPLE CHOICE UNIT TEST 2 - *White Fang*

I. Matching

___ Gray Beaver   A. Weedon Scott's friend/helper

___ Cherokee   B. Is saved by White Fang

___ Beauty Smith   C. Saved White Fang

___ One Eye   D. The gray cub

___ Mit-sah   E. White Fang's Indian master

___ Jim Hall   F. Gray Beaver's son

___ Weedon Scott   G. White Fang's father

___ White Fang   H. Dog in Gray Beaver's camp

___ Judge Scott   I. Tormented & used White Fang to make money

___ Kiche   J. White Fang's mother; she-wolf

___ Lip-lip   K. Tried to kill the judge

___ Matt   L. Bulldog who fought White Fang

White Fang Multiple Choice Test 2 Page 2

II. Multiple Choice

1. Where does this story take place?
    a. In Greenland
    b. In the far North
    c. In Iceland
    d. In Russia

2. What happened when Bill tried to save One Ear?
    a. Bill barely managed to save One Ear.
    b. One Ear turned on him.
    c. One Ear saved them both.
    d. Both Bill and One Ear were eaten.

3. What confused the gray pup?
    a. The snow
    b. The floor
    c. The white wall
    d. The lynx

4. What happened to One Eye?
    a. The she-wolf got mad and killed him.
    b. He went away as was the custom of the male wolves.
    c. The lynx killed him.
    d. Hunters killed him.

5. How did White Fang differentiate man from beast?
    a. Man fought with clubs and guns.
    b. Man had fire.
    c. Man smelled different.
    d. Man walked on his hind legs.

6. What was the "crime of crimes"?
    a. Leaving man
    b. Stealing from man
    c. Disobeying man
    d. Biting man

7. What fighting technique did White Fang successfully use?
    a. Feigning
    b. Surprise
    c. Holding the throat
    d. Clawing

White Fang Multiple Choice Test 2 Page 3

8. Why did White Fang return to Gray Beaver?
    a. Life with man was much easier than life in the wild.
    b. Gray Beaver came after him and forced him to return.
    c. He couldn't find his mother.
    d. He was wounded.

9. Why was White Fang afraid of hands?
    a. They often held clubs and whips.
    b. They were always moving.
    c. They looked strange.
    d. He didn't understand them.

10. What did White Fang think of the "white gods"?
    a. He liked them.
    b. The thought they were not very smart.
    c. They were more powerful than the Indians.
    d. He trusted them.

11. Why did Gray Beaver sell White Fang?
    a. He was tired of retrieving White Fang from the wild.
    b. He wanted whiskey.
    c. He decided to move away and couldn't take White Fang with him.
    d. White Fang was nothing but trouble for him.

12. Why did White Fang always win his fights?
    a. He fought only smaller, domesticated dogs.
    b. The experiences of his life had made him a skillful fighter.
    c. Beauty wouldn't take a fight he didn't know White Fang could win.
    d. The fights were "fixed."

13. Why didn't Matt kill White Fang?
    a. He missed; White Fang got away.
    b. He was out of ammunition.
    c. He didn't have the nerve.
    d. He realized White Fang was too smart to kill.

14. What did White Fang do when Weedon Scott left in the spring?
    a. He would not eat and became sick.
    b. He went to look for his master.
    c. He carried on "as usual."
    d. He ran away back to the wild.

White Fang Multiple Choice Test 2 Page 4

15. What was so important about White Fang's snuggling?
    a. It kept Weedon Smith warm.
    b. It showed his total confidence in Weedon Scott.
    c. It helped him get well.
    d. It was his way of saying he was lonely.

16. Why wouldn't White Fang fight the Collie?
    a. His fighting days were over.
    b. He didn't want to kill the Judge's dog.
    c. His instincts would not let him fight a female.
    d. He was afraid of her.

17. Why did White Fang kill the dogs at the crossroads?
    a. The dogs had taunted White Fang, and given permission to fight.
    b. They attacked the Judge.
    c. The dogs attacked the collie.
    d. They took his food.

18. Why did White Fang leave the injured Weedon Scott in the woods?
    a. He went to chase a rabbit.
    b. He got confused.
    c. He didn't realize his master was injured.
    d. His master told him to go.

19. What happened to White Fang?
    a. He eventually returned to the wild.
    b. He died from wounds he got while saving the judge.
    c. He lived happily ever after with the Scotts and the collie.
    d. He was put to sleep.

White Fang Multiple Choice Test 2 Page 5

III. Vocabulary

___ 1. Vicariously   A. fulfilled by the substitution of another person or thing

___ 2. Impelled   B. trying to get into another's good will

___ 3. Prodigious   C. confident

___ 4. Indomitable   D. predatory excursion

___ 5. Defiant   E. be desirable of, longing for unlawfully

___ 6. Indulgently   F. willing to provoke, challenging to fight

___ 7. Allegiance   G. swearing, speaking irreverently

___ 8. Dissipated   H. permeated, flowed through

___ 9. Ulterior   I. irrepressible; invincible

___ 10. Pervaded   J. huge, enormous

___ 11. Ingratiating   K. loyalty

___ 12. Foray   L. toughness

___ 13. Covetous   M. vanished, scattered

___ 14. Tenacity   N. unmanageable

___ 15. Sanguinary   O. futile, pointless

___ 16. Blasphemy   P. driven or urged forward, pressed upon

___ 17. Epitomized   Q. summarized, condensed

___ 18. Guise   R. obligingly; tolerantly

___ 19. Vainly   S. behavior

___ 20. Incorrigible   T. undisclosed; hidden

ANSWER SHEET - *White Fang*
Multiple Choice Unit Tests

I. Matching	II. Multiple Choice	IV. Vocabulary
1. ___	1. ___	1. ___
2. ___	2. ___	2. ___
3. ___	3. ___	3. ___
4. ___	4. ___	4. ___
5. ___	5. ___	5. ___
6. ___	6. ___	6. ___
7. ___	7. ___	7. ___
8. ___	8. ___	8. ___
9. ___	9. ___	9. ___
10. ___	10. ___	10. ___
11. ___	11. ___	11. ___
12. ___	12. ___	12. ___
	13. ___	13. ___
	14. ___	14. ___
	15. ___	15. ___
	16. ___	16. ___
	17. ___	17. ___
	18. ___	18. ___
	19. ___	19. ___
		20. ___

ANSWER KEY - *White Fang*
Multiple Choice Unit Tests

Answers to Unit Test 1 are in the left column. Answers to Unit Test 2 are in the right column.

I. Matching	II. Multiple Choice	IV. Vocabulary
1. C E	1. A B	1. A A
2. K L	2. C D	2. O P
3. F I	3. A C	3. F J
4. A G	4. B C	4. B I
5. I F	5. D A	5. K F
6. L K	6. B D	6. G R
7. B C	7. A B	7. E K
8. D D	8. B A	8. R M
9. E B	9. C A	9. L T
10. H J	10. D C	10. I H
11. J H	11. A B	11. C B
12. G A	12. C B	12. Q D
	13. C D	13. J E
	14. B A	14. H L
	15. C B	15. P C
	16. D C	16. D G
	17. D A	17. M Q
	18. B D	18. S S
	19. A C	19. N O
		20. T N

UNIT RESOURCE MATERIALS

BULLETIN BOARD IDEAS - *White Fang*

1. Save one corner of the board for the best of students' *White Fang* writing assignments.

2. Display maps and pictures of the Northern wilderness.

3. Make a bulletin board showing articles and pictures of wild animals which have been brought into captivity.

4. Title the board: LAW OF THE WILD: EAT OR BE EATEN. Place pictures of animals eating other animals. (Example: a frog eating a fly, a snake eating a frog, a badger eating a snake, a wolf eating a badger, etc.) You could have students bring in pictures of animals eating other animals. Let students post their own pictures on the bulletin board. This could be an alternate introductory activity.

6. If you are teaching *White Fang* and *Call of the Wild* together, display a chart on which students can write-in their observations comparing and contrasting Buck and White Fang.

7. Use a story line to show White Fang's transformation from being "wild" to being "civilized."

8. Do a bulletin board promoting your local zoo. (I"m sure they'll be glad to give you information!) You might consider taking Polaroid pictures of your local zoo for your bulletin board.

9. Take one of the word search puzzles from the extra activities section and with a marker copy it over in a large size on the bulletin board. Write the clue words to find to one side. Invite students prior to and after class to find the words and circle them on the bulletin board.

10. Do a bulletin board about careers in forestry, wilderness management, zoology, veterinary science, or other related fields.

11. Make a bulletin board listing the vocabulary words for this unit. As you complete sections of the novel and discuss the vocabulary for each section, write the definitions on the bulletin board. (If your board is one students face frequently, it will help them learn the words.)

MORE ACTIVITIES - *White Fang*

1. Use some of the related topics (noted earlier for an in-class library) as topics for research, reports or written papers, or as topics for guest speakers.

2. Take a trip to your local zoo.

3. Research and discuss careers which deal with wildlife (vet., game warden, zoologist, biologist, etc.)

4. Have students find poems or lyrics to songs which relate to *White Fang*

5. Have students research background information about animals on the endangered species list.

6. Show the film *White Fang* after you have completed reading the novel in class. Have students evaluate the movie and compare/contrast it with the book. If the students have tried writing a chapter into a scene in a play, you may wish to discuss how the problems they encountered in changing the form were handled in the movie.

7. Have students design a book cover (front and back and inside flaps) for *White Fang*.

8. Have students design a bulletin board (ready to be put up; not just sketched) for *White Fang*.

9. Have students do a research project about the domestication of animals. The assignment is to choose an animal people have as pets and to research and write a report about how the animal was domesticated. If the animal is still considered "wild" (snakes, monkeys, some birds, etc.) students should research and write a report about how the animal is captured and what steps have to be taken to convert it to a "pet."

10. Take students camping in the "wild."

11. Have students plan a camping trip to the remote areas of the far north.

12. Have a guest speaker come in or do a mini-unit to discuss survival techniques.

EXTRA ACTIVITIES

One of the difficulties in teaching a novel is that all students don't read at the same speed. One student who likes to read may take the book home and finish it in a day or two. Sometimes a few students finish the in-class assignments early. The problem, then, is finding suitable extra activities for students.

One thing that helps is to keep a little library in the classroom. For this unit on *White Fang*, biographical information about Jack London would be interesting for some students. You can include other related books and articles about wolves, pets, domestication of animals, Naturalism in writing, careers related to animals, Darwinian theories, survival skills, or articles of criticism about Jack London's work. Books by other writers who use naturalism might be of interest to some of your students.

Other things you may keep on hand are puzzles. We have made some relating directly to *White Fang* for you. Feel free to duplicate them.

Some students may like to draw. You might devise a contest or allow some extra-credit grade for students who draw characters or scenes from *White Fang*. Note, too, that if the students do not want to keep their drawings you may pick up some extra bulletin board materials this way. If you have a contest and you supply the prize (a record album or something like that perhaps), you could, possibly, make the drawing itself a non-refundable entry fee.

The pages which follow contain games, puzzles and worksheets. The keys, when appropriate, immediately follow the puzzle or worksheet. There are two main groups of activities: one group for the unit; that is, generally relating to the *White Fang* text, and another group of activities related strictly to the *White Fang* vocabulary.

Directions for these games, puzzles and worksheets are self-explanatory. The object here is to provide you with extra materials you may use in any way you choose.

WORD SEARCH - *White Fang*

All words in this list are associated with *White Fang*. The words are placed backwards, forward, diagonally, up and down. The included words are listed below the word searches.

```
K W C W G N M P Q M P F Z C E B R P E S W P Q Y
N K H E H C P L A G P S L X J N N D C Y T A M D
R E V A E B Y A R G N I T O O F I C E B E T L X
K O T C K A T T S F V A N B W C T M M M U I Q L
L G K C L R F V E N J E F Q K D C E A C W R W W
N O D O N G E H C D E N J E L E E T E F F P N Z
S U N C H I C K S Y A K H H T I M S Y T U A E B
Y E B E L I T W E H E Y C A A I P A S P H S N H
M R C L K J A S C E E C H I N L H L J E O V M M
H T O A H L F S N H O W L S H D L W I O L I F E
D C P L R U K A P I C Z O E U C S I M P R B F D
L X O L W T N R T R X B N L B R F S B X K M Z Q
L X K O V S A G C T A R N S F Y P N M G M S J C
Y O R W K E J H E L Y N X M E A T R G C W Z E X
G X N C F O E J F R K J G Z D P T N I O V G M Z
X L B D T R O P F Z Y H H W B Z I T N S D C D T
Q X B S O N D L H Z N N G Z F T F S C U E Z F F
W D T K Y N Z K K K C L C H I Q N R J K W C C P
Y V E Z Q W K B F R W Y X B M V T Y W K W D Q P
N E S D W E E D O N S C O T T L N M J M Z B P P
```

ALONE	FAN	KEENAN	PUP
BEAUTY SMITH	FATTY	KICHE	SHE WOLF
BET	FEAR	KLOOKOOCH	SNOW
BILL	FOOTING	LAWS	SPRANG
BITING	GAP	LIFE	SUN
BLESSED WOLF	GRAY BEAVER	LIP LIP	SURPRISE
BURN	HALL	LONDON	TAME
CHEROKEE	HANDS	LOVE	TEETH
CHICKENS	HATE	LYNX	TRACES
CHICKS	HENRY	MAJOR	WALL
COLLIE	HOWL	MEAT	WEEDON SCOTT
DAY	HUNGER	MEN	WHITE FANG
DICK	ICE	MOOSE	WILD
EYE	INSTINCT	ONE	
FAMINE	JUDGE	ONEEYE	

KEY: WORD SEARCH - *White Fang*

All words in this list are associated with *White Fang*. The words are placed backwards, forward, diagonally, up and down. The included words are listed below the word searches.

```
                        P         F       E         W
               E          A G     L     N D Y     A     D
          R E V A E B Y A R G N I T O O F I C E B E T   L
            O T     A       S     A N   W C T M   M U I   L
      L     C L       E N   E F   K D   E A     W R
            O   O N   E H   D E     E L E E T F F P N
      S U N C H I C K S Y A K H H T I M S Y T U A E B
          E   E L I T W E H E Y C A A I P A S P H S N
      M   C L K   A S     E E     H I N L H L J E O
      H   O A H L F S N H O W L S H D L W I O L I F E
          C     R U   A P I       O E U C S I M P R B
            O       T N R T R     N L   R     B B
      L       O     A G C T A R       F   P
                O   K E   H E L Y N X M E A T R G   W     E
                  N   F O E     R     G         N I O   G
                    D   R O                   I   N S D
                      O     L             T     S   U E
                        K   N     K         I         J
                      E                   B
                E       W E E D O N S C O T T
```

ALONE	FAN	KEENAN	PUP
BEAUTY SMITH	FATTY	KICHE	SHE WOLF
BET	FEAR	KLOOKOOCH	SNOW
BILL	FOOTING	LAWS	SPRANG
BITING	GAP	LIFE	SUN
BLESSED WOLF	GRAY BEAVER	LIP LIP	SURPRISE
BURN	HALL	LONDON	TAME
CHEROKEE	HANDS	LOVE	TEETH
CHICKENS	HATE	LYNX	TRACES
CHICKS	HENRY	MAJOR	WALL
COLLIE	HOWL	MEAT	WEEDON SCOTT
DAY	HUNGER	MEN	WHITE FANG
DICK	ICE	MOOSE	WILD
EYE	INSTINCT	ONE	
FAMINE	JUDGE	ONEEYE	

CROSSWORD - *White Fang*

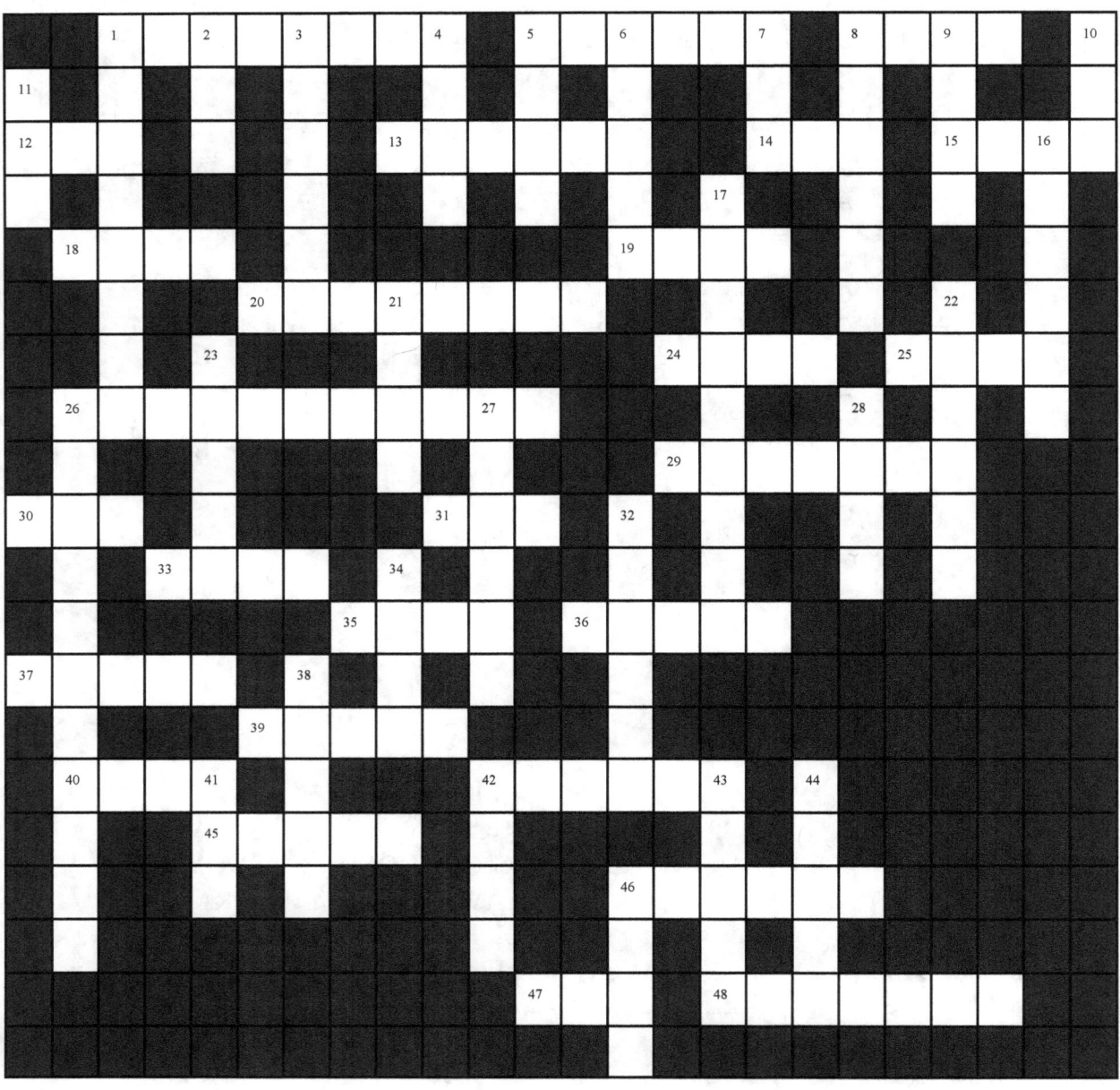

CROSSWORD CLUES - *White Fang*

ACROSS

1. White Fang surprised the Judge by not eating them
5. A man was absolutely forbidden
8. Rules
12. Sight organ
13. She has White Fang's pups
14. Baby dog
15. Opposite of death
18. Wolves do this at the moon
19. He tried to kill the judge
20. Natural inclination
24. Strong feeling of affection
25. Fire did this to White Fang's nose
26. Tormented and used White Fang
29. Foot placement
30. These use clubs and guns to fight
31. Spread out shape
33. Apprehensive feeling
35. What White Fang felt towards Beauty
36. The she-wolf
37. Bill's partner who survived
39. Dog eaten by wolves in the beginning of the story
40. Opposite of tame
42. Gray Beaver's boy
45. By yourself
46. Author
47. It gives light and warmth
48. White Fang's mother

DOWN

1. Bull dog who fought White Fang
2. Frozen water
3. Tim who brought Cherokee to fight White Fang
4. White flakes
5. Henry's partner who got eaten
6. White Fang used them to rip meat
7. Space between
8. Dog that picked fights with White Fang at the Indian camp
9. It confused the gray cub
10. Single
11. Wager
16. A time of no food
17. Gray Beaver's wife
21. Opposite of wild
22. Feeling caused by empty stomach
23. White Fang saved him from Jim Hall
26. Name Scott women gave White Fang
27. Apparatus used to harness dogs to sleds
28. A deerhound who belonged to Judge Scott
32. Gray cub found them when he fell through the pine trunk
34. Weedon's friend and helper
38. White Fang killed him for trying to take his meat
41. Opposite of night
42. Carnivores eat it
43. White Fang was afraid of these because they controlled whips and clubs
44. Large animal providing meat
46. She wolf killed a mother one

CROSSWORD ANSWER KEY - *White Fang*

MATCHING QUIZ/WORKSHEET 1 - *White Fang*

___ 1. KLOOKOOCH   A. What White Fang felt towards Beauty

___ 2. HATE   B. Opposite of death

___ 3. SPRANG   C. Gray Beaver's Wife

___ 4. ALONE   D. Frozen water

___ 5. ICE   E. Tim who brought Cherokee to fight White Fang

___ 6. KICHE   F. By yourself

___ 7. FOOTING   G. White Fang saved him from Jim Hall

___ 8. FAN   H. The she-wolf

___ 9. SURPRISE   I. White Fang used this fighting tactic

___ 10. BURN   J. Foot placement

___ 11. HENRY   K. Bill's partner who survived

___ 12. JUDGE   L. Spread out shape

___ 13. CHEROKEE   M. Opposite of wild

___ 14. CHICKS   N. It gives light and warmth

___ 15. LYNX   O. Fire did this to White Fang's nose

___ 16. COLLIE   P. Bull dog who fought White Fang

___ 17. TAME   Q. Gray cub found them when he fell through the pine trunk

___ 18. SUN   R. She has White Fang's pups

___ 19. KEENAN   S. She wolf killed a mother one

___ 20. LIFE   T. Lept

KEY: MATCHING QUIZ/WORKSHEET 1 - *White Fang*

C 1. KLOOKOOCH   A. What White Fang felt towards Beauty
A 2. HATE   B. Opposite of death
T 3. SPRANG   C. Gray Beaver's Wife
F 4. ALONE   D. Frozen water
D 5. ICE   E. Tim who brought Cherokee to fight White Fang
H 6. KICHE   F. By yourself
J 7. FOOTING   G. White Fang saved him from Jim Hall
L 8. FAN   H. The she-wolf
I 9. SURPRISE   I. White Fang used this fighting tactic
O 10. BURN   J. Foot placement
K 11. HENRY   K. Bill's partner who survived
G 12. JUDGE   L. Spread out shape
P 13. CHEROKEE   M. Opposite of wild
Q 14. CHICKS   N. It gives light and warmth
S 15. LYNX   O. Fire did this to White Fang's nose
R 16. COLLIE   P. Bull dog who fought White Fang
M 17. TAME   Q. Gray cub found them when he fell through the pine trunk
N 18. SUN   R. She has White Fang's pups
E 19. KEENAN   S. She wolf killed a mother one
B 20. LIFE   T. Lept

MATCHING QUIZ/WORKSHEET 2 - *White Fang*

___ 1. KLOOKOOCH   A. Tim who brought Cherokee to fight White Fang

___ 2. JUDGE   B. Spread out shape

___ 3. KEENAN   C. Apparatus used to harness dogs to sleds

___ 4. ONE EYE   D. White Fang used them to rip meat

___ 5. INSTINCT   E. Henry's partner who got eaten

___ 6. WALL   F. White Fang saved him from Jim Hall

___ 7. SURPRISE   G. Rules

___ 8. BITING   H. A man was absolutely forbidden

___ 9. LOVE   I. White Fang's father

___ 10. TRACES   J. It confused the gray cub

___ 11. FAN   K. Strong feeling of affection

___ 12. FAMINE   L. Gray Beaver's Wife

___ 13. MOOSE   M. White Fang surprised the Judge by not eating them

___ 14. CHICKENS   N. White Fang used this fighting tactic

___ 15. LAWS   O. Opposite of tame

___ 16. MAJOR   P. Natural inclination

___ 17. BILL   Q. Large animal providing meat

___ 18. WILD   R. A time of no food

___ 19. SHE WOLF   S. White Fang killed him for trying to take his meat

___ 20. TEETH   T. White Fang's mother

KEY: MATCHING QUIZ/WORKSHEET 2 - *White Fang*

L 1. KLOOKOOCH		A. Tim who brought Cherokee to fight White Fang
F 2. JUDGE		B. Spread out shape
A 3. KEENAN		C. Apparatus used to harness dogs to sleds
I 4. ONE EYE		D. White Fang used them to rip meat
P 5. INSTINCT		E. Henry's partner who got eaten
J 6. WALL		F. White Fang saved him from Jim Hall
N 7. SURPRISE		G. Rules
H 8. BITING		H. A man was absolutely forbidden
K 9. LOVE		I. White Fang's father
C 10. TRACES		J. It confused the gray cub
B 11. FAN		K. Strong feeling of affection
R 12. FAMINE		L. Gray Beaver's Wife
Q 13. MOOSE		M. White Fang surprised the Judge by not eating them
M 14. CHICKENS		N. White Fang used this fighting tactic
G 15. LAWS		O. Opposite of tame
S 16. MAJOR		P. Natural inclination
E 17. BILL		Q. Large animal providing meat
O 18. WILD		R. A time of no food
T 19. SHE WOLF		S. White Fang killed him for trying to take his meat
D 20. TEETH		T. White Fang's mother

JUGGLE LETTER REVIEW GAME CLUE SHEET - *White Fang*

SCRAMBLED	WORD	CLUE
KDIC	DICK	A deerhound who belonged to Judge Scott
LWLA	WALL	It confused the gray cub
EETHT	TEETH	White Fang used them to rip meat
EGHNWIFAT	WHITE FANG	The gray cub
UDGEJ	JUDGE	White Fang saved him from Jim Hall
STAHMI	MITSAH	Gray Beaver's boy
NIEKHSCC	CHICKENS	White Fang surprised the judge by not eating them
FLOEWHS	SHE WOLF	White Fang's mother
NXYL	LYNX	She wolf killed a mother one
OOEMS	MOOSE	Large animal providing meat
LBLI	BILL	Henry's partner who got eaten
TMEA	MEAT	Carnivores eat it
ICKEH	KICHE	The she-wolf
AFIEMN	FAMINE	A time of no food
TMTA	MATT	Weedon's friend and helper
ASGPRN	SPRANG	Lept
EON	ONE	Single
AEHT	HATE	What White Fang felt towards Beauty
OEILLC	COLLIE	She has White Fang's pups
ENLAO	ALONE	By yourself
UNGERH	HUNGER	Feeling caused by empty stomach
YDA	DAY	Opposite of night
EFLWLOSSDEB	BLESSED WOLF	Name Scott women gave White Fang
CNTINTSI	INSTINCT	Natural inclination
ASLW	LAWS	Rules
ALLH	HALL	He tried to kill the judge
UNS	SUN	It gives light and warmth
LLIIPP	LIP LIP	A dog that picked fights with White Fang at the Indian Camp
OWNS	SNOW	White flakes
AFRE	FEAR	Apprehensive
ETB	BET	Wager
EMTA	TAME	Opposite of wild
EYEOEN	ONE EYE	White Fang's father
AHSTIBTYEMU	BEAUTY SMITH	Tormented and used White Fang

White Fang Review Game #7 Clue Sheet Continued

SCRAMBLED	WORD	CLUE
KOKCOOOHL	KLOOHOOCH	Gray Beaver's Wife
EFIMAN	FAMINE	A time of no food
UISRSEPR	SURPRISE	White Fang used this fighting tactic
YDA	DAY	Opposite of night
ANF	FAN	Spread out shape
NSU	SUN	It gives light and warmth
VLEO	LOVE	Strong feeling of affection
GFNOOTI	FOOTING	Foot placement
SCHKCI	CHICKS	Gray cub found them when he fell through the pine tree trunk
SNWOTCEDETO	WEEDON SCOTT	He saved White Fang
YEE	EYE	Sight organ
LDWI	WILD	Opposite of tame

VOCABULARY RESOURCE MATERIALS

VOCABULARY WORD SEARCH - *White Fang*

All words in this list are associated with *White Fang*. The words are placed backwards, forward, diagonally, up and down. The included words are listed below the word searches.

```
Z T N F F Y H Q V H E P N S Y E G A L E T U T Q
S C Y C A C I F F E R F Y H U J D K B K C T K I
W U Z R L S Q M F H C T F E N O G E K A E P N M
P R O F U S E L Y D I S S I P A T E D L S T C Z
W F T T S S L C P M L M M Z C I T I B A E H P Z
V F B S I Q H A N D B P P Z C A T A P R V Y E S
S Y G U K U L E D A U E K E C O C O M I Q R A D
I M G B R P C E O D I B F M L A V I M L C N E J
B N O I I G S R E S D G G U L L N E O I G E B P
T X D T N S E N I E T N E P D A E T T U Z F R D
C E A O E E T O G C I E M L B D C D I O S E E P
G N N R M L V N N T R I N L L Y L N J P U T D M
T Y P A Y I I I A I U E Y T D A A E M L A S G Z
V P R L C P T N T I N L T T A R G R D C T T M F
O A G A M I I A M A F G T I Y T Y T I U Q E H K
Y W I I T M T U B Y B E M E C Q I D M Z P L Z Y
Z R B N L I T Y T L R L D F R E N O Z V Z M N N
X M G U L C O M R X E I E O M I N O U S T V T R
Z V C S I Y Y N K D L Q A X V Z O C Z S H H Z M
P O N D E R O U S Q L B Z D L E S R E V D A F H
```

ABASHED	DISSIPATED	IMPLACABLE	PONDEROUS
ADVERSE	EFFICACIOUS	IMPUDENTLY	PRECIPITOUS
ALLEGIANCE	EFFICACY	INDOMITABLE	PROFUSELY
ANTIPATHY	ENMITY	INEVITABLE	RETICENCE
BEFUDDLED	EPITOMIZED	INTERMINABLY	SANGUINARY
BURGEONING	EQUITY	MYRIAD	SMOTE
CIRCUITOUS	FORAY	OMINOUS	TENACITY
COVETOUS	GUISE	OPPRESSED	TUTELAGE
CULMINATING	GYRATIONS	OSTENTATIOUS	ULTERIOR
DEFIANT	IMPELLED	PALPITANT	VAINLY
DICTUM	IMPINGED	PERVADED	VINDICATED

KEY: VOCABULARY WORD SEARCH - *White Fang*

All words in this list are associated with *White Fang*. The words are placed backwards, forward, diagonally, up and down. The included words are listed below the word searches.

```
                    Y         E     S   E G A L E T U T
        S   Y C A I F F E     F Y   U   D   B           I
            U   R                 T F   O   E A E       N
        P R O F U S E L Y D I S S I P A T E D L S T
            F   T   S   C P M   M M   C I   I B A E H
              B   I     A N   B P P   C A T A P R V   E S
        S     U   U L E D A U E   E   O C O M I   R A D
        I M G   R P C E O D I   F   L A V I M   C N E
            N O I I G S R E S D G G U L L N E O I G E     P
        T   D T N S E N I E T N E P D A E T T U Z   R D
            E A O E E T O G C I E M L B D   D I O S E E P
        G N N R M L V N N T R I N L L   L N   P U T D
        T Y P A Y I I I A I U E Y T   A A E     A S
        V P R   C P T N T I N L T   A R       D C   T
        O A   A M I I A M A F G T I Y T Y T I U Q E H
              I I T M T U B Y B E   E C   I D           Y
              N L I T Y   L R L D   R E N O
              U L C O         E I E O M I N O U S
            C   I Y   N         A   V   O C   S
        P O N D E R O U S         D   E S R E V D A
```

ABASHED	DISSIPATED	IMPLACABLE	PONDEROUS
ADVERSE	EFFICACIOUS	IMPUDENTLY	PRECIPITOUS
ALLEGIANCE	EFFICACY	INDOMITABLE	PROFUSELY
ANTIPATHY	ENMITY	INEVITABLE	RETICENCE
BEFUDDLED	EPITOMIZED	INTERMINABLY	SANGUINARY
BURGEONING	EQUITY	MYRIAD	SMOTE
CIRCUITOUS	FORAY	OMINOUS	TENACITY
COVETOUS	GUISE	OPPRESSED	TUTELAGE
CULMINATING	GYRATIONS	OSTENTATIOUS	ULTERIOR
DEFIANT	IMPELLED	PALPITANT	VAINLY
DICTUM	IMPINGED	PERVADED	VINDICATED

VOCABULARY CROSSWORD - *White Fang*

VOCABULARY CROSSWORD CLUES - *White Fang*

ACROSS
1. Struck sharply or heavily
3. Under the guardianship
7. White Fang killed him for trying to take his meat
8. Predatory excursion
10. Reaching the highest point
12. Opposite of night
13. Behavior
14. Frozen water
16. Futile, pointless
18. Sight organ
19. Single
21. Overpowered, overburdened
23. Undisclosed; hidden
25. It gives light and warmth
27. Able to resist attack, invincible
30. What White Fang felt towards Beauty
31. Opposite of wild
32. Carnivore's eat it
36. Admonishment; rebuking; reprimanding
39. White Fang was afraid of these because they controlled whips and clubs
40. Confident
42. Swearing, speaking irreverently
43. Baby dog
44. Rules

DOWN
2. Hostility, opposition
3. Toughness
4. Summarized, condensed
5. Capable of producing the desire effect
6. Living in a pack, not solitary
7. A countless number, innumerable
9. Fairness
10. Roundabout; indirect
11. Sporadic movements
12. Willing to provoke, challenging to fight
15. Irrepressible; invincible
17. Clashed, dashed against
20. Blossoming, growing
22. Force, energy
24. Strong feeling of affection
26. These use clubs and guns to fight
28. Opposed to; against
29. Opposite of death
31. White Fang used them to rip meat
33. It confused the gray cub
34. An authoritative saying, ruling
35. Spread out shape
37. A deerhound who belonged to Judge Scott
38. He tried to kill the judge
41. Space between

VOCABULARY CROSSWORD - *White Fang*

137

VOCABULARY WORKSHEET 1 - *White Fang*

___ 1. Driven or urged forward, pressed upon
    A. incorrigible   B. guise   C. impelled   D. uncompromisingly

___ 2. A countless number, innumerable
    A. prodigious   B. intrepidity   C. myriad   D. equity

___ 3. Disgraced
    A. abasement   B. efficacy   C. vindicated   D. antipathy

___ 4. Strike sharply or heavily
    A. allegiance   B. incorrigible   C. culminating   D. smote

___ 5. Massive and awkward
    A. ponderous   B. indomitable   C. circuitous   D. epitomized

___ 6. Be desirable of, longing for unlawfully
    A. interminably   B. ostentatious   C. foray   D. covetous

___ 7. Forward in behavior, bold-faced
    A. impudently   B. adverse   C. allegiance   D. ingratiating

___ 8. Summarized, condensed
    A. abasement   B. pervaded   C. epitomized   D. indomitable

___ 9. Lavishly, exuberantly
    A. befuddled   B. profusely   C. reticence   D. gyrations

___ 10. Behavior
    A. vainly   B. interminably   C. guise   D. antipathy

___ 11. Ever present
    A. ingratiating   B. ubiquitous   C. dictum   D. impelled

___ 12. Fairness
    A. foray   B. vicariously   C. equity   D. ulterior

___ 13. Obligingly; tolerantly
    A. impudently   B. indulgently   C. efficacy   D. impregnable

___ 14. Trembling, throbbing
    A. profusely   B. palpitant   C. precipitous   D. burgeoning

___ 15. Swearing, speaking irreverently
    A. gyrations   B. palpitant   C. blasphemy   D. myriad

___ 16. Huge, enormous
    A. ponderous   B. circuitous   C. prodigious   D. vicariously

___ 17. Proved to be just or valid
    A. vindicated   B. myriad   C. interminably   D. indomitable

___ 18. Very steep
    A. vainly   B. precipitous   C. dissipated   D. profusely

___ 19. Bound to happen
    A. vindicated   B. inevitable   C. palpitant   D. efficacious

___ 20. An authoritative saying, ruling
    A. dictum   B. abasement   C. dissipated   D. myriad

KEY: VOCABULARY WORKSHEET 1 - *White Fang*

__C__ 1. Driven or urged forward, pressed upon
    A. incorrigible   B. guise   C. impelled   D. uncompromisingly

__C__ 2. A countless number, innumerable
    A. prodigious   B. intrepidity   C. myriad   D. equity

__A__ 3. Disgraced
    A. abasement   B. efficacy   C. vindicated   D. antipathy

__D__ 4. Strike sharply or heavily
    A. allegiance   B. incorrigible   C. culminating   D. smote

__A__ 5. Massive and awkward
    A. ponderous   B. indomitable   C. circuitous   D. epitomized

__D__ 6. Be desirable of, longing for unlawfully
    A. interminably   B. ostentatious   C. foray   D. covetous

__A__ 7. Forward in behavior, bold-faced
    A. impudently   B. adverse   C. allegiance   D. ingratiating

__C__ 8. Summarized, condensed
    A. abasement   B. pervaded   C. epitomized   D. indomitable

__B__ 9. Lavishly, exuberantly
    A. befuddled   B. profusely   C. reticence   D. gyrations

__C__ 10. Behavior
    A. vainly   B. interminably   C. guise   D. antipathy

__B__ 11. Ever present
    A. ingratiating   B. ubiquitous   C. dictum   D. impelled

__C__ 12. Fairness
    A. foray   B. vicariously   C. equity   D. ulterior

__B__ 13. Obligingly; tolerantly
    A. impudently   B. indulgently   C. efficacy   D. impregnable

__B__ 14. Trembling, throbbing
    A. profusely   B. palpitant   C. precipitous   D. burgeoning

__C__ 15. Swearing, speaking irreverently
    A. gyrations   B. palpitant   C. blasphemy   D. myriad

__A__ 16. Huge, enormous
    A. ponderous   B. circuitous   C. prodigious   D. vicariously

__A__ 17. Proved to be just or valid
    A. vindicated   B. myriad   C. interminably   D. indomitable

__B__ 18. Very steep
    A. vainly   B. precipitous   C. dissipated   D. profusely

__B__ 19. Bound to happen
    A. vindicated   B. inevitable   C. palpitant   D. efficacious

__A__ 20. An authoritative saying, ruling
    A. dictum   B. abasement   C. dissipated   D. myriad

VOCABULARY WORKSHEET 2 - *White Fang*

___ 1. SACRILEGIOUS   A. Trembling, throbbing

___ 2. INEVITABLE   B. Admonishment; rebuking; reprimanding

___ 3. SMOTE   C. Endlessly

___ 4. PALPITANT   D. Forward in behavior, bold-faced

___ 5. IMPUDENTLY   E. Roundabout; indirect

___ 6. CHASTISEMENT   F. Able to resist attack, invincible

___ 7. INTERMINABLY   G. Fearless, bold

___ 8. IMPELLED   H. Strike sharply or heavily

___ 9. ULTERIOR   I. Under the guardianship

___ 10. IMPLACABLE   J. Clashed, dashed against

___ 11. IMPREGNABLE   K. Violation of something sacred

___ 12. RETICENCE   L. Bound to happen

___ 13. TUTELAGE   M. Swearing, speaking irreverently

___ 14. IMPINGED   N. Driven or urged forward, pressed upon

___ 15. MYRIAD   O. Baffled, puzzled

___ 16. CIRCUITOUS   P. Reserve; restraint

___ 17. BEFUDDLED   Q. Vanished, scattered

___ 18. DISSIPATED   R. Undisclosed; hidden

___ 19. INTREPIDITY   S. A countless number, innumerable

___ 20. BLASPHEMY   T. Unrelenting, cannot be appeased

KEY: VOCABULARY WORKSHEET 2 - *White Fang*

K	1. SACRILEGIOUS	A. Trembling, throbbing
L	2. INEVITABLE	B. Admonishment; rebuking; reprimanding
H	3. SMOTE	C. Endlessly
A	4. PALPITANT	D. Forward in behavior, bold-faced
D	5. IMPUDENTLY	E. Roundabout; indirect
B	6. CHASTISEMENT	F. Able to resist attack, invincible
C	7. INTERMINABLY	G. Fearless, bold
N	8. IMPELLED	H. Strike sharply or heavily
R	9. ULTERIOR	I. Under the guardianship
T	10. IMPLACABLE	J. Clashed, dashed against
F	11. IMPREGNABLE	K. Violation of something sacred
P	12. RETICENCE	L. Bound to happen
I	13. TUTELAGE	M. Swearing, speaking irreverently
J	14. IMPINGED	N. Driven or urged forward, pressed upon
S	15. MYRIAD	O. Baffled, puzzled
E	16. CIRCUITOUS	P. Reserve; restraint
O	17. BEFUDDLED	Q. Vanished, scattered
Q	18. DISSIPATED	R. Undisclosed; hidden
G	19. INTREPIDITY	S. A countless number, innumerable
M	20. BLASPHEMY	T. Unrelenting, cannot be appeased

VOCABULARY JUGGLE LETTER REVIEW GAME CLUES - *White Fang*

SCRAMBLED	WORD	CLUE
RGDYLOOSIIUP	PRODIGIOUSLY	Extraordinary, enormously
SERAEVD	ADVERSE	Opposed to; against
NBOGNRIUEG	BURGEONING	Blossoming, growing
TEIMZIPDEO	EPITOMIZED	Summarized, condensed
AGNNIIARTGIT	INGRATIATING	Trying to get in another's good will
ESMPBYALH	BLASPHEMY	Swearing, speaking irreverently
EEABMRLGNPI	IMPREGNABLE	Able to resist attack, invincible
EGBIROLRNCII	INCORRIGIBLE	Unmanageable
NSMIUOO	OMINOUS	An ill omen
YFORA	FORAY	Predatory excursion
ERCNCEEIT	RETICENCE	Reserve; restraint
EOTSM	SMOTE	Strike sharply or heavily
ROLTERUI	ULTERIOR	Undisclosed; hidden
FEICACYF	EFFICACY	Force, energy
NTNILYDLGEU	INDULGENTLY	Obligingly; tolerantly
IATNILOMEDB	INDOMITABLE	Irrepressible; invincible
UOOPDSENR	PONDEROUS	Massive and awkward
MBLATININRYE	INTERMINABLY	Endlessly
MNITGUICALN	CULMINATING	Reaching the highest point
IYENMT	ENMITY	Hostility, opposition
YIQTUE	EQUITY	Fairness
ATTANIYPH	ANTIPATHY	Dislike, opposition
DVEARPED	PERVADED	Permeated, flowed through
AEMIPBLACL	IMPLACABLE	Unrelenting, cannot be appeased
TUDCMI	DICTUM	An authoritative saying, ruling
ERYNTITIPD	INTREPIDITY	Fearlessness, boldness
BINATELEIV	INEVITABLE	Bound to happen
ASTMSTENCHIE	CHASTISEMENT	Admonishment; rebuking; reprimanding
TNGROSIYA	GYRATIONS	Sporadic movements
ITOAOESSTNU	OSTENTATIOUS	Vain, pomp, ambitious display
ICAEDTNIDV	VINDICATED	Proved to be just or valid
ANYTTECI	TENACITY	Toughness
FUCFECIAISO	EFFICACIOUS	Capable of producing the desired effect
MDEIPELL	IMPELLED	Driven or urged forward, pressed upon
ESTUIRPPICO	PRECIPITOUS	Very steep
PIDEMNGI	IMPINGED	Clashed, dashed against
LYVAIN	VAINLY	Futile, pointless
BIUTUQOSUI	UBIQUITOUS	Ever present

www.ingramcontent.com/pod-product-compliance
Lightning Source LLC
Chambersburg PA
CBHW051414070526
44584CB00023B/3421